The Happiness of Finding Wisdom

Introduction: 3

1 **Reaching Your Potential:** 5
It's finally time: 5
Your talents: 7
Prophetic vision: 8
The Rampart Vision: 12
The Prophetic VISION of the House of God: 16
How awesome is this place: 16
Passionate Desire: 20
Diligence: 23
Wise Decisions: 25
Cautions to Remember: 27

2 **Wisdom Builds the House:** 37
What Wisdom Does & Says: 30
Wisdom's Two Sides: 32
Building our "Sure House:" 34
Dimensions: 37
The blueprint: 38
Building to finish: 42
That house: 39
Boundaries: 40
Building to finish: 43
Wisdom's actions: 44
Terms for wisdom: 46

3 The 1st step—Fear: 47

   The House of Godliness: 48
      Foolish people don't fear: 50
      The house itself: 55
      Two minds, two wives: 56

4 The 2nd Step—Knowledge: 61

   Learning How to "Get wisdom:" 61
      Knowing God was lost: 64
      The devil's plan: 65
   The Carnal Mind Doesn't Know: 63
   Mastery over Ungodly Activities: 67
      Accurate knowledge creates the furniture for your house: 79

5 The 3rd Step—Understanding: 83

   Establishing the House: 83
   Living Foolishly: 86
   The Ability to Understand Comes into the Soul: 90
   Essay: 92
   All Three: 97

6 The 7 Pillars of Wisdom: 94

   The Structure of the House: 94
      The 7 pillars: 95
      A review of Wisdom's dinner: 103

7 The Kinds of Wisdom: 109

   Finding the Correct Wisdom: 109
      The Hebrews' house: 112
      Building unto perfection: 114
      The happiness of a dream fulfilled: 116

Bibliography: 118

THE HAPPINESS OF FINDING WISDOM

*"Live life, then, with a due sense of responsibility,
not as men (and women) who do not know
the meaning and purpose of life —
But as those who do.
Make the best uses of your time,
despite all the difficulties of these days."*
Ephesians 5:15-16 (Phillips)

By
Pastor Kluane Spake Ph.D.

Spake World Outreach Detachment
SWORD, Inc.

Rightly Dividing Series
ISBN # 0-9704433-3-1

2nd printing

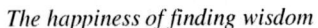

The happiness of finding wisdom

To my children: Shawn Miller, Roddy, David, & Dyanna Spake; and to my grandchildren: Jordan, Dorian, Angel, & Amber —
that they may obtain great happiness in finding wisdom.

Cover design & mountain drawing by Kluane Spake

INTRODUCTION

THIS TIME

I was determined to change "this time."

There must be happiness for me somewhere. Finally, I made my formal declaration of, "I mean it — this is it. I will become that person I'm supposed to be." But days lengthened on into years and nothing really happened. I tried... just couldn't make it.

Why is it that we can't find contentment? Why do we fail? What's wrong? We want easy steps and then we forget to do them. We blame evil conditions on the devil, a circumstance, or someone else. But blame never changes the situation. Truth is, God gave us the responsibility of directing our lives. If we're honest with ourselves as individuals, we will realize that each one of us has the capacity to choose happiness or misery.

GET HAPPY:

Proverbs gives us the biggest clue to happiness; **Happy is the man that findeth wisdom...** (Prov. 3:13a). Happiness. Who could ask for more? Here we're told that a person who finds wisdom is happy. In other words, happiness is a by-product of finding wisdom.

What is happiness? It means different things to different people. While the world searches for happiness in drugs, sex, and entertainment – people are still sad. Even worse, believers often get discouraged and slip back to their old ways. Of course, there's always the confusion of our words trying to express the phenomena what makes us "feel" happy. We know that momentary merriment quickly fades, while long lasting happiness comes only from the ability to receive from God and to wisely respond to His intentions. He has only the best to give us.

The Tree of Life stands offering the reality of LIFE to all who will partake of it. Jesus, our Tree of Life, sits in the center of our garden on the throne of our heart – His blood still provide the power to fully enable us to embody His nature and blessings. Now's the chance for you to decide to change forever by finding wisdom. Finding THE wisdom that brings happiness is the focus of this book.

So here we stand this day at the door of the outer court of our Temple, seeking entrance into a better life. Yet, no one can give us admission, and we can't sneak in the back door. It takes *preparation* for a Christian to enter into this new dimension of happiness, and a great deal of importance must be attached to this truth of preparation. If we aim for greater happiness then we must understand what it is... What makes me happy? Why does it make me happy? Do I really want to be happier? Now listen, if we really want to be happy, then we have to become wise. Where do we start? If we lack wisdom, James

Introduction

tells us to **"Ask of God"** (James 1:5). And so we ask today, in all sincerity.

Happiness is not a goal in itself, but a result of *being*. We can't own happiness, or possess it, but we can "be" happy. Happiness is not life's pursuit, but rather life's essence. We are happy when we find wisdom. We're happy when our life has relevance and potency. Happiness is the awesome ability to do the work of God. Happiness is the expression of entirely living in wisdom and resonating with the frequency of heaven.

> God gives us the position of "sonship" and "adoption" (Gal. 4:5). That means we are heirs of all things – including wisdom. All believers, both men and women, have the right of inheritance as "sons." That adoption occurs when we're come of age (see Romans 8:14, **"For as many as go in the Spirit of God, they are the sons** (grown up sons) **of God."** But, this inheritance isn't ours unless we walk in it in every area of our life – body, soul, and spirit. There can be no happiness unless we learn to recognize the activity of the presence of the eternal God within our being. Wisdom completes and fulfills our life with the happiness and contentment of *becoming* and *being* who we were created to be.

So how do we find this wisdom that makes us happy? Second Timothy tells us that the Holy Scriptures are able to make us wise. In this book, we'll study a lot of scripture. We'll learn the necessity of becoming a people intent upon challenging the present "weak and beggarly elements" (Gal 4:9) of this world. We will see how wisdom forms the basis for our lives, and we will learn to use this wisdom for our happiness and well-being.

The book of Proverbs likens finding wisdom to building a house on a sure foundation. Wisdom alone builds (1 Kings 6:7, Prov 3:7-12) through right choices that create a life worth living. Happiness <u>is</u> possible when we become aware of our life and where we're going. We have to open our eyes and not just allow whatever comes along to happen.

We have to <u>wake up!</u> (Rom. 13:11) And this waking up can be uncomfortable. If you do what you always have done, then you will get what you've always gotten.

The Happiness of Finding Wisdom

FINDING WISDOM

IT'S FINALLY TIME –

Yes, it's time to wake up.

We must awaken to an apprehension of life. But, life isn't lived in one fell swoop (or "one swell foop" – as my kids would say). It isn't defined by a single event, but rather comprises a process of continuous growth and becoming. As believers, we're not just passing through this lifetime to get to another, but we're living NOW in eternity present. If there's any one right answer to finding success and happiness, it's learning to enjoy this here and now process of growth and change. That change continues with us. Through healthy planning, we participate in our destiny instead of accidentally wandering and stumbling over missed opportunities. The intentional process of getting to that precise result brings success and happiness.

Happiness acknowledges the inner revelation of our individual purpose and direction. Happiness drives toward maturity and the fulfillment of our responsibilities in life to ourselves, others, and to our environment. Happiness isn't just making money or becoming popular. True, profound happiness and the joy of well-being is derived from becoming what you can become: kind and good, secure and committed, faithful and God fearing. Yes, we can be quickened with an awakened personality and loving intentions.

Yet we often fail to get there. These non-physical virtues do not exist in a dimension that our rational mind can detect. Soooo — we almost never appreciate ourselves in the process of being and becoming. We generally spend our time unable to distinguish between the real potential and the illusion of our mind. Yet, we must be discerning in order to build a real place for ourselves and become real people.

We also almost never realize that our choices determine the quality of life we live and the contribution we have on others. Life is a gift that we can't create, but we can direct. It's sacred. What we are born with is God's gift to us. Each of us only has one short lifetime on earth – our upcoming future can become our gift back to God.

Our past tells us how it's been so far. Learning to assess how we've spent that lifetime isn't easy. One way to begin to know who we really are is to examine how we've used our time. It's much like the old song, "The Way We Were." While singing, perhaps we

FINDING WISDOM
It's finally time –

can logically take a look at ourselves. Are we disorganized? Spoiled? Discouraged? Perhaps we're like Phyllis Diller, who joked about how she kept a desk drawer full of "get well" cards. Then, if unexpected company caught her sleeping late and still in her pajamas, she could strew the cards about her entry, and claim that she had the flu – "Please excuse the mess – just couldn't make it to work today."

Of course, perfectionism is the enemy on the other extreme. We'll talk again about that later. But, the point is, we don't impress God through vain self-works. We can never EARN blessings -- but can only accept them as gifts. It's not what I DO that matters -- but rather, who I AM.

However, our Godly inspired effort is the natural outcropping of a sincerely planted seed. We need to act upon God's directions. Remember, we labor WITH God and not FOR Him. He's our life-source on earth. He alone is omnipotent and divine. The Holy Spirit allows us to hook arms with the Lord and walk toward our common goal in true synergy -- the sum total of the whole becoming greater than the sum of its parts. Synergistic living is birthed from the passionate longing to know and understand God's will for your life.

The reason most of us begin to find life boring or meaningless is because we have not determined God's ultimate goals or purposes toward which we can aim our lives. There's a lack of meaning. When we live only for today, then today can become unendurable. When each day is lived to the fullest, we experience the catalyst dynamic of fulfilling purpose.

Happiness is a state of mind that is filled with positive thoughts of internal contentment from abiding in that fixed upright order.

> ***Finally deciding to change and then doing something to start that change, is a monumental incident that needs to be celebrated.***

The Happiness of Finding Wisdom

FINDING WISDOM.
It's finally time –

WORN OUT EXCUSES FOR BAD HABITS:
>I have too much to do. I don't have the energy.
>I don't have enough time. Nobody helps me. Nobody cares.
>I'm sick and weak. Let someone else do it.
>I don't want to. Why bother?
>I'll start tomorrow.
>I had to stay up all last night.
>It's too hot, too cold, too late, too early, etc.

No one likes to talk about the life that got away. The scenario's too familiar – you meant to keep those goals, pay those bills, take that class… there just wasn't time.

> *But don't forget, He... won't let you get by with sloppy living.*
> *Your life is a journey you must travel with a deep consciousness of God.*
> *It cost God plenty to get you out of that dead-end, empty-headed life*
> *you grew up in. He paid with Christ's sacred blood..."* (1 Pet. 1:8-19 Message)

YOUR TALENTS:

Happiness? You know, humanity has always searched for that magic answer of finding true satisfaction. Thankfully, God has already placed the answers to success within you. Way down deep, you know that there's no "one" answer… but there are many things that will help you accomplish your destiny. You just have to recognize your talents, and then allow them to spring forth. These answers lie hidden in God's purpose – the 'how and why' He created you.

> *Happiness = Becoming what we are supposed to become —*
> *discovering God's plan and accomplishing it.*

**Write about what do you love to do. What do you do well? (You won't get much out of this book if you don't do the assignments.)

Do you recognize your reason for life? A talent can be described as that which you can do easily, that others may find difficult. *The test of your life is how well you use your talents* (Matt. 25:20). Not only do you need to accept your gifts and talents, but also you need to love them – the Lord does! He accepts you. You are your natural and spiritual talents – that's you. You can't be someone else. Few people ever fully see with that single eye (Matt. 6:22, Luke 11:34). But, you'll soon see how this illumination increases as you allow yourself room to breathe and grow.

The Happiness of Finding Wisdom

FINDING WISDOM
Prophetic vision:

If we feel that this process of "being a success" depends on us, then we frantically live for ourselves and our self-driven plans. If we assume that it's all up to God, then we probably won't live up to our part of the deal. We're co-laborers. Remember — **"A man's mind plans his way, but the Lord directs his steps"** (Prov. 16:9 RSV).

1. Your talents point you to your destiny. Doing unnecessary things counts for very little. Doing big things that don't contribute to your meaning in life also count for little. Do what matters.
2. Your God-given talents are what you need to succeed; you won't have to strive.
3. There are eternal consequences to the use of talents.
4. Moses' rod wouldn't work until he lifted it (Ex. 4:20). Your ability won't produce until you use your talents.

Surely, the Lord in His mercy gives gifts and then frees you to use them. If you decide to join up with Him, then He will see that your joint-plans happen.

- Choose to use your talents to productively cause Kingdom–advancing works to go forward in the earth.
- Acknowledge that success does not happen by your own power, but only when you become the agent of God, participating with His plan.
- Realize that to continually waste time is a sin against vision.

PROPHETIC VISION:

I spent most of my life not knowing how to be happy, what to do, or how to get things done. Anger and disappointment became a routine that caused things to not work out. I did my best, but nothing happened. Repeated failure overwhelmed me. I felt like life owed me an explanation because I was trapped into a short-circuited lack of progress. My motivation was to please others. But, deep inside, I knew that I had to move beyond dysfunction and victimization. How? I was frightened of the answer.

Recently, I saw a picture of the Lord playing jacks with a friend named Susan. The jacks represented the way her life was going— just like she planned. Susan methodically threw out the jacks and never missed catching the ball — until the game was finished — and

FINDING WISDOM
Prophetic vision:

she won. She loved winning all the time. Suddenly, God scooped up the silvery jacks and held them in His closed fist. He then explained that He would like the next turn... and He would throw out the jacks for her to play the next game. Soon, the jacks went far and wide. She was alarmed, as I had been, to lose control of the future. His plan was far greater and more complex than hers. She couldn't imagine that it could be possible to have her life positioned on such a grand scale.

Finally, we begin to understand... we've been like children building our own castle in the sand according to our plan and our ways. Soon the vast ocean rushes towards our schemes, washing away the sandy foundations, lapping over the walls. "We have followed too much the devices and desires of our own hearts..." Now, it's time to release that old sand castle – it can't survive — no matter how much prayer goes forth. The tiny castle is not the right one. Every house will be tested when the storms come. It's time to arise and build from a new schematic. Build on the Lord, His tides pull us toward Him and carry us great distances with His forceful current. From beneath the surface of the sea, the water itself redistributes new sand dunes in strange new places.

> *Vision = the ability to clearly see into the progressive direction of the will of God.*

In each of us, much remains to be healed. No one is totally whole. Everyone is in process. The realization of needing to restructure our life may be instantaneous, but the pursuit of that goal is a life-long process. Embracing wisdom means that you decide to become conscious of the areas of your soul (personality) that need to be healed. Only then can you begin to reshape your responses. You and you alone give God permission to start working on what needs to be done. Your responsible choices cultivate and nourish your garden and allow the growth inside.

Listen, if you don't care what happens, then any ol' road will do. Whatever will be, will be – as they say. If you don't want to hit a target, then don't aim at all. Go ahead, play golf in a parking lot – you don't need the holes. Shoot arrows into the air. Why not? People without purpose have no reason to care. Without revelation, people perish. They cast off restraint (Prov. 19:18). Vision gives purpose. Central vision could be defined as the expressed prophetic purpose of your life -- not just what you should DO, but also the character and nature you were created to express.

WITHOUT PROPHETIC VISION:

Without a vision, people perish. This famous verse of Proverbs 29:18 has often been misquoted because the word "vision" has taken on new meaning since AD 1611. The Hebrew literally means, "Where there is no prophetic vision, the people perish." The

The Happiness of Finding Wisdom   1-9

FINDING WISDOM
Prophetic vision:

RSV is right --"Where there is no prophecy."[1] Our response to our prophetic (God given) vision, determines our future. The meaning of "the people perish" also has many significations which may apply here.

> **The people are made stripped bare, made ashamed**, exposed to danger because of lack of prophetic vision.
>
> **The people rebel**, because they know no better. As several translations say, "they cast off restraint."
>
> **The people are idle**, they do nothing to any good purpose, for want of instruction what to do and how to do it.
>
> **They are scattered** as sheep having no shepherd. They are scattered from their duty to God (2 Chron. 15:3,5).

They perish; they are destroyed for lack of knowledge, (Hos. 4:6).[2] The Hebrew word for *perish* means to wander in confusion. If you don't identify your prophetic vision, then you'll wander and let whatever comes along just happen. Without vision, your life's direction could be adversely defined by your woundedness or by coincidence.

We must have prophetic vision. Vision brings foresight with insight. Vision sees where God wants to take us. This prophetic vision is not necessarily seeing a supernatural or angelic apparition, or hearing an audible voice concerning the future. We don't have to be translated to a heavenly realm to receive prophetic vision. Most of the time it comes naturally out of the acknowledgment of our talents.

How you respond to your present existence TODAY determines your future.

You need perseverance in prayer (Lk. 18:1), expecting to receive clarity of vision. It's the receiving of answers that's important, not just letting the request be known. It's not wrestling with Satan, nor banging on closed gates. God's ready to activate positive action in you. Suddenly, life's no longer a struggle, but a privilege.

---

1. The Wycliffe Bible Commentary, Electronic Database. (c) 1962 by Moody Press.
2. Initial source, Matthew Henry Commentary.

FINDING WISDOM.
Prophetic vision:

Embracing vision and deliberate purpose drives you into progressive changes. Aiming toward vision always solves your decisions — it orders your day. It determines your life's agenda. What you do, who you really are, and even your personal style reflect the divine purpose of your life. Vision can be detected in your true passion, talents, and responses. Once found, it defines the design for your life and the dream in your heart. Expect a prophetic revelation of the Kingdom that will change the your destination.

__Arise from depression and prostration in which circumstances have kept you – rise to a new LIFE! Shine (be radiant with the glory of the Lord), for your light has come, and the glory of the Lord has risen upon you!__
(Is. 60:1 AMP).

WISDOM IS A FORCE:

Wisdom *is* the power by which we journey to our highest spiritual and emotional wholeness. That wholeness of wisdom manifests itself in a positive outlook, controlled emotions, willing obedience, readiness to withstand opposition, eager enthusiasm, and a love for people. It brings all the personal elements into harmony with God's image and likeness. (Gen. 1:26). We finally realize that God no longer placates our idolatry or allows us to conceive of Him in our image. God's plan becomes foremost. He's all that stands behind door number three. There's nothing else.

We must have no identity outside of Christ.

The realization of identity starts small, but we're not supposed to despise the days of small beginnings. We don't have to stay small. Abraham Lincoln wrote on the back of a shovel with coal – but he moved on. There's power to expand our lives — but only if we believe God's Word. Remember, God won't respond to our discouragement and He won't confirm our fleshly desires. Bur, He does respond to our faith in His plan.

We must see the reality of the unseen. Faith is our response to God's tug. Like the Samaritan woman who left her waterpot to evangelize her city, we respond with action to accomplish what was already established in heaven. Jesus gave us "all authority." There's nothing greater than that.

Check list toward getting there:
- Decide what God wants for you (vision & purpose).
- Come into agreement with that plan and be radically obedient to the Holy Spirit when given particular instructions (Rm. 8:26-27).

The Happiness of Finding Wisdom

FINDING WISDOM
The Rampart Vision

- Believe when you pray. Believe you receive. (Matt. 11:24, Jn. 16:23, Matt. 21:22).
- Find rest. Strife and confusion can shut you down.
- Cast down wicked imagination (2 Cor. 10:4) and works of the old nature.
- Find God's applicable promises and meditate on them.
- Wake up! Be thankful (Phil. 4:6). Worship. Receive the will of God.
- Hope in the future. Maintain your confession of faith.
- Act on the plan. Mental assent is the most subtle enemy; it agrees but doesn't act.

Every dream follows the law of seedtime and harvest. All day, every day, you plant and tend your future into your garden. That planted vision must be watered constantly. It is never in competition with another person's vision. But the vision is forward and direct for you. There's a special fragrance about knowing who you are --a quality of calmness and unshakable confidence. People will suddenly want to be around you. Your targeted life will also affect the course of others around you for good.

But life is worth nothing unless I use it for doing the work assigned me by the Lord Jesus –
(Acts 20:24 TLB).

THE RAMPART VISION

Let's continue the idea of diligently finding your vision by examining several translations of what Habakkuk said about the rampart (NKJ, TLB, NIV, ASV combined). 2:1 **I will climb my <u>watchtower</u>** (station or better. "<u>stand</u> myself on the ramparts") **now and wait to** (look forth to) **see what answer** (what He will speak with me) **God will give to my <u>complaint</u>** (or what answer I am to give concerning this request).

RAMPART:

The Hebrew word translated as rampart means encirclement; but the general sense of the word is that of the front line of defense that protected a city. [1] (Of course, we see the typology that Jesus Christ is the High Tower that we can run into.) A rampart, watchtower, or

---

[1]. Some definitions from Nelson's Illustrated Bible Dictionary) (Copyright (C) 1986, Thomas Nelson Publishers)

The Happiness of Finding Wisdom

FINDING WISDOM
The Rampart Vision

battering ram tower consisted of an elevated and often portable structure that was positioned next to the city wall. The watchman would peer over the city wall and observe the attacking enemy. From this protected vantage point, he would then tell his soldiers how to gauge a counter attack.

STAND

Habakkuk had a "complaint" about the adverse circumstances that he faced. He decided to "stand" there on the rampart. Vines Expository Dictionary explains various ways of standing. One may "stand" for a definite purpose at a particular spot: "...stand upon the rampart..." From the basic meaning of this verb comes the definition "to be established, immovable, and standing upright" on a single spot. The verb suggests being "immovable," or "to abide and remain."

Standing is synonymous to the meaning we have discussed before when God put Adam into the Garden of Eden to "dress it and to <u>keep it</u>" (Gen. 2:15). Proverbs uses this word of guarding "to watch" one's mouth (Prov. 13:3), the tongue (Ps. 34:13), and the lips (Ps. 141:3). It's our job to guard our garden vision.

Why did Habakkuk stand? So that he could keep watch and guard. In this case, guarding signifies a watchman fulfilling the responsibility of guarding. We also see that standing/guarding is also mentioned in Genesis 26:5, "Because that Abraham obeyed my voice, <u>*and kept my charge,*</u> my commandments, my statutes, and my laws."

WAIT

Many times it seems that God is silent. Waiting sometimes seems to take forever. It took Israel forty years to climb out of the desert, Jesus waited all his life until He was 30, and it took 50 days from the crucifixion to the coming of the Holy Spirit. My waiting through limbo times is no longer a problem when I can have faith without ambiguity and the assurance that God is working "in the meantime."

This word is also translated "set," which implies something or someone that will not fall over. Like the crouching catcher waiting to catch the baseball, Habakkuk would wait and not be moved.

WATCH

<u>*The Happiness of Finding Wisdom*</u>

FINDING WISDOM
The Rampart Vision

Tsapah ^6822^ is found in the text of the Hebrew Bible about 37 times. The meaning in this context is "to anxiously lean forward with anticipation" with a purpose of seeing.

TO SEE, PERCEIVE:

Habakkuk stood guard on the rampart watching to *see* what God would say. The verb ra'ah ^7200^ means, "to perceive, get acquainted with, gain understanding, or examine..." This verb has several further extended meanings. For example, this idea of seeing pertains to our spiritual vision.

SPEAK:

Here we focus on the content (meaning) of what was said — the actual "words" themselves. It was the "word of the Lord" that came to Habakkuk as he stood and waited.[1] The question here is, will you stand and wait until you see what God will say to you?

The standing, waiting, watching, and seeing gave Habakkuk the answer. And what did God answer? Here it comes in the next verse! VISION! Hab. 2:2, **And Jehovah answered me, and said, 'Write the vision,** (write my answer on a billboard) **and make it plain upon tablets** (large and clear)**, that he may run that readeth it.** So that anyone can read it at a glance and rush to tell the others.'

This activity of recording vision develops the reason WHY you will do something later – it becomes your conviction – the driving force to your actions.

**Begin to write your answers now as you read. Let this be a time to spark ideas about what you desire. Make it plain. Now's the time to write a philosophy of life. Can you find Scriptures that encourage you in this quest? What do you want to accomplish in this lifetime? In one year? In one month? Ask yourself, what gives me joy and contentment? Why was I born? What is my vision? What gives me energy? When do I have a sense of achievement? What do I hate to do? What will I do today? What moves me forward beyond my limits? **

YOUR GODLY VISION IS A PLAN WAITING TO BECOME A REALITY.

The Godly vision creates a reference point -- what you steer toward. Clarification comes when each area of life directs itself toward the same ultimate goal. Your vision is like the great North Star — you know where to go and what to do by looking at it.

---

1. All definitions condensed from Vine's Expository Dictionary of Biblical Words, ibid.

- If you need to find your way again, you can adjust your course toward the vision.
- Other things may change, but the North Star remains fixed in the center – and everything rotates around it.
- Lives that are fixed upon Godly vision have a constant sense of the magnetic pull of direction.
- The North Star (vision) establishes location as a personal coordinate.

IT TAKES TIME TO BUILD A DREAM:

To dream – the godly imagination hitches your soul to a star.
To work – the price of accomplishment.
To think – the source of renewed power.
To play – the secret of staying young.
To read – the foundation of obtaining knowledge.
To understand – the action of realization.
To worship – the door to fear and reverence.
To love – the one sacrificial sacrament of life.
To laugh – the way to ease the load.
To see—to recognize beauty and appreciate it more clearly.
To plan – the secret of getting something accomplished while still having time for the more important things.[1]

THE PROPHETIC VISION OF THE HOUSE OF GOD:

How awesome is this place! This is none other than the house of God, and this is the gate of heaven
(Gen. 28:17).

Many studies say that 87% of our nation is dysfunctional. That's almost inconceivable! It's a huge identity crisis. Most people are insecure and have little sense of self-worth.

---
1. Expanded from an unknown source.

The Happiness of Finding Wisdom

FINDING WISDOM
The prophetic VISION of the house of God:

They've been like Jacob, who had no personal vision. He just wanted to be like his brother. More important than anything else was that Jacob needed his dad's approval. But his dad loved Esau (Gen. 25:28).

Perhaps you have often felt like Jacob -- trying to behave like someone else in order to measure up or deserve your birthright. Jacob was caught in a trap of performance; he didn't know who he was. He was first born and the legal inheritor; but he couldn't believe it.

Eventually, Jacob fulfilled the meaning of his name – liar and supplanter. His idol, Esau had a better life, and Jacob tried to copy him. Jacob tried to produce something of his self-nature. Esau was unaware of the value of his inheritance, and tried to sell it for a pot of soup. Often, we do not realize what we possess. We believe what others tell us — and deny who we are. Like Jacob and Esau, we're balanced in the tension place of finding God's will for our lives and not walking in the flesh. It's only through a yielded and open heart that we can receive the revelation of who we really are.

> No one else can replicate who you are. Of the six billion on earth, no one else has the same fingerprints, the same memories, the same voiceprint, the same eye print, the same DNA, or the same mind. No dead person has had your same uniqueness either!

"Who are you?" That's what the blind father said as he fondled Jacob's fur covered arms. And, that's also what Boaz said to Ruth. "Who are you?" To answer that question, we need prophetic vision – to discover who we are. God sees beyond the skins of the animals on our arms – the pretenses and facades. He looks into our heart… under our skin. He loves us. We don't have to perform or mimic someone else to get His acceptance. We don't have to work to get approval.

God has a plan!

Later on in life, Jacob wanted to be blessed. He wrestled with the angel of God and wouldn't let him go. It took determination on Jacob's part to alter his life. Finally, at age 72, the Lord finally got the Jacob nature (*liar, supplanter*) out of him. Let's look at what happened: Jacob had traveled from Beersheba to Harran and stayed the night sleeping outdoors on stones. Genesis 28 tells how Jacob dreamed of a ladder set on earth that reached to heaven. Angels ascended and descended on it. The ladder represents the connection between heaven and earth. Jesus told the disciples, "**Behold… The kingdom of God is <u>near you</u>**" (Luke 10:9 NIV). He told Nathaniel that the ladder ascended and descended "on the Son of Man!"

The Happiness of Finding Wisdom

FINDING WISDOM.
The prophetic VISION of the house of God:

BEHOLD

<u>Behold</u> = it's time to see! That kind of beholding must come through revelation. Behold, God's kingdom comes on earth as it is in heaven. That hallowed kingdom appears because we release it. Upon our decree, it comes violently advancing (Matt. 11:12) against oppositional forces that cannot peacefully coexist with it. It never retreats. Beholding connects us with heaven and earth. Our prayers then unify with heaven (the place where God's presence dwells.) and press into forward activity.

It was there at Bethel (see also Jdg. 20:18-27). that God re-connected and re-confirmed the covenant promises and blessings previously made to Abraham and Isaac. It was there at the time of coupling, that the Lord God changed Jacob's name, giving him a new identity and personality.

From then on, Israel limped (God touched the hollow place) – and his daily walk was different. Through the internal relationship of connecting with God's plan, we become whole. God works inside. He lives in us. We're not what we do or what we preach. But out of our innermost being (hollow place, place of conception) we find the authentic signature of Truth... Who we are. We become who we're meant to be. We do the things that are no longer external but ETERNAL.

When Israel woke up he said, **"Surely the Lord is in this place.... How <u>awesome</u> is this <u>place</u>! This is none other than the <u>house</u> of God and this is the <u>gate</u> of <u>heaven</u>."** Then he poured oil on his stone pillow and called that place Bethel, which means the "House of God."

HOW AWESOME IS THIS PLACE"
FEARFUL and AWESOME

This same word repeats= Strong's Dictionary defines # 3372 yare' as to revere, be made afraid, stand in awe, fear. This word is used concerning a person "standing in awe." This does not mean to be afraid, but to reverence -- whereby an individual recognizes the power and position of the individual revered and renders him proper respect... So Jacob said of Bethel: "How *awesome* is this place!"

PLACE

Strong's # 4725 *maqowm* standing, i.e. a spot ... This noun is used to signify a sanctuary — i.e., a "place" of worship" in our body, mind, or in this world.

The Happiness of Finding Wisdom

FINDING WISDOM
The prophetic VISION of the house of God:

"THIS IS NONE OTHER THAN THE HOUSE OF GOD."
HOUSE

Webster's defines the house as follows: "A place or house of worship, especially a synagogue. A place devoted to a special purpose." Matthew Henry defines the house: "He that is joined to Christ is one spirit. He is yielded up to him and is hereupon possessed and inhabited by His Holy Spirit. This is the proper notion of a house or temple – a place where God dwells and that is sacred to His use." Jesus is the Father's <u>house</u> (Jn. 14:2).

HOUSE = *bayit* ^1004^ "First, this noun denotes a fixed, established structure as a "permanent dwelling place." *Bayit* also represents a place of worship or "sanctuary. A third use of *bayit* sometimes refers to the place where something or someone dwells or rests. In other words, this could mean, this place "in me" where God dwells.

So far, by using these definitions, we can re-word this verse and hear Jacob say, "I stand in awe over this place of worship where God dwells inside of me right now..."

"THE GATE OF HEAVEN."
GATE

Sha'ar ^8179. Basically, this word represents a structure closing and enclosing a large opening through a wall, or a barrier through which people and things pass to an enclosed area. The "gates" were the place where local courts convened.

Building this house of God becomes the <u>gate of heaven</u> — the entrance into heavenly communion and God's nature. The *gate* inside of us becomes the entrance into eternal concerns. Through these gates we connect with God. The Psalmist says, **Lift up your heads, O you gates and be lifted up, you everlasting doors! Then the King of glory shall come in.** Yes, believers are God's gates of entrance upon the earth.

- Our wise prophetic decree appeals, "Let us go into the GATE of the house of the Lord."
- Our <u>gates</u> are praise (Is. 60:18). When our praise gates are opened wide, we will possess the gates of the enemy (Gen. 24:60). Now, don't gloss over this point. The abiding presence of God inside means that the enemy's gate of hell shall not (and can not) prevail against us (Matt.

The Happiness of Finding Wisdom

FINDING WISDOM.
The prophetic VISION of the house of God:

16:18). Every precise purpose of God will happen, regardless of opposition.

- The wise wife stands at the GATE. We become the GATE of entry.
- Jeremiah stands at the GATE to prophetically declare a decree that all people coming into this gate should worship the LORD! (7:2).
- Jesus is the GATE for the sheep (Jn. 10:7).

HEAVEN

Shamayim ^8064^ is the usual Hebrew word for the "sky." This realm is where birds fly. This area, high above the ground but below the stars and heavenly bodies, is often the location of visions: <1 Chr. 21:16>. "Heaven" is described as the dwelling place of God.[1]

Collecting the understanding of these words amplifies the meaning of Jacob's remark, "How awesome is this place of worship where God dwells and is enthroned in that which is living and breathing inside of me right now." Most certainly this place (of experience) is the permanent dwelling place (sanctuary, house), the resting place of God. It is the gate (the opening) though which God can connect (and pass to give spiritual revelations and visions) to me."

Worship connects us in our earthly state to God's presence.
— His Kingdom comes in us. We are His house.

Know ye not that <u>ye are</u> (plural – corporately) **the temple of God… for the temple of God is holy, which <u>temple ye are</u>.** (KJV) You are the tabernacle -- with a rent veil! You're positioned to manifest the fullness of Christ in your sphere of influence. The altar isn't at the front of your church building – it's in your heart. The only priest is you. The only sacrifices going on are the fruit of your lips giving thanks. The only vespers ceremony is the presence of God walking and talking with you at the break of day.

2 Cor. 6:16 KJV … **For <u>ye are</u> the temple of the living God; as God hath said, I will dwell in them** (take up permanent residence), **and walk in them** (as in the garden); **and I will be their God, and they shall be my people.**

Jeremiah 29:4-5 NIV … the God of Israel, says… **Build houses and settle down; plant gardens and eat what they produce.** The believer builds according to God's plan.

---

[1] Condensed definition from Vine's Expository Dictionary of Biblical Words) (Copyright (C) 1985, Thomas Nelson Publishers)

The Happiness of Finding Wisdom

FINDING WISDOM
Passionate Desire

1 Pet. 2:5 KJV **Ye also, as lively stones** (pieces of a greater structure), **are built up a spiritual house**…

PASSIONATE DESIRE

Vision allows people to perceive themselves differently -- they begin to visualize the house that they are to become. Where they may have previously misperceived themselves as lacking, fundamentally less than others, isolated, fragmented, or cut off and alone — now they find themselves to be part of a whole work and a piece of a master plan.

If you find out what your part is in this plan, then suddenly you have purpose –the *why* of what you do. Your vision is your *purpose (the house that you will build).* Jesus died to give you that reason for LIFE.

Finding purpose creates the passionate desire and the determination to accomplish that dream. Finding purpose in life is the stuff that goals are made out of; it passionately drives us forward. We can't even talk more about accomplishing our purpose/vision until we uncover *desire*. We're not talking about sitting around and gently wanting something – like a hot fudge sundae. Far greater is the craving to do the precise will of God. Desiring to accomplish our purpose is that very golden key to winning. We must desire the ultimate product of our prophetic vision more than the pleasures of the moment. That's what Moses did (Heb. 11:25). Will you desire to know the great plan for your life? Will you connect to God and find His purpose? Will you desire to accomplish it? Without desire you can't achieve your soul's potential.

Wisdom fixes her eyes on the prize -- rather than the obstacles. Wisdom learns to make choices on what could be, rather than what is. Wisdom forgoes immediate results anticipating that the overall vision leads to worlds not yet imagined. Responding to Godly *desire* is the day weakness is cast away forever — and the people of Zion emerge a strong city (Is. 26:1-2).

Desire = a passionate longing, a want, a craving. A magnetic-like attraction (As the deer panteth for the waterbrook — Ps. 42:1).

FUNCTION OF GODLY DESIRE:

- Godly desire is the force of expectation that motivates us toward prophetic vision.

The Happiness of Finding Wisdom

- Expectation motivates and propels us to our purpose: it gives meaning and direction. In most decisions, our choice is (1) a meaningful activity or (2) a less-meaningful activity. If we operate in Godly desire, then this decision-making process is easy.
- Desire builds strong philosophical values in a correct manner.
- Desire gives the central theme from which our life makes sense. Our individual activities and goals are not random, but rather extensions from our overall life-theme.
- Desire grants inner strength and momentum. If our lives move toward our desire, we experience peace and courage even when we encounter struggles and suffering.
- Accomplishing meaningful desire gives satisfaction. Even if the results are not perfect, we know that "we fought the good fight" (2 Tim. 4:7).

David *desired* the Lord so much that he groaned, **Lord, all my desire is before thee; and my groaning is not hid from thee** (Ps. 38:9). Not only do we desire, but also the Spirit of God *desires* so much for us to find our right path that He intercedes for us with *groanings* that cannot be uttered (Rom. 8:26). Our success comes only because He actively intercedes concerning the working of our lives.

As our minds become filled with accomplishing His desires, we change progressively from glory to glory, to greater levels. The Lord actually puts inside of us the desire of our heart (Psa. 37:4). I used to believe that meant that I could have whatever I wanted (desired). But now I understand that even greater than that, God gives me *His* desires. He plants His desires within my nature.

1 King 10:13 speaks of great desire, **And King Solomon** (a type of God) **gave unto the queen of Sheba** (a type of the bride) **all her desire, whatsoever she asked**... God wants to enhance our particular desires.

Our greatest desire should be to find the wisdom of God. That's what this book is about — obtaining the wisdom of God. Proverbs 3:15 says, **She** (wisdom) **is more precious than rubies: and all the things thou canst desire are not to be compared unto her**. (KJV).

Ps 145:16 **Thou openest thine hand, and satisfiest the desire of every living thing**. (KJV)

FINDING WISDOM
Passionate Desire

Prov 13:12 **Hope deferred maketh the heart sick: but when the <u>desire</u> cometh, it is a tree of life**. (KJV) Accomplishing desire creates the fruit that the Husbandman waits to receive. God offered the Tree of Life in the garden, and He offers it to us today. That GOD-LIFE consummates our desires. No longer bound in mediocrity and defeat, we arise in conscious awareness that we have taken on the character and likeness of the Almighty. A new mentality irresistibly aims us forward into the unlimited future. We BECOME His desire.

What is God's desire for you? Where is your Promised Land? It is the place where God enthrones upon the LIFE HE breathes into you. Finding and fulfilling that ultimate desire brings satisfaction and happiness. Think about the fact that no one has ever existed like you. You have special and unique abilities, interests, and experiences that make you – you. Have you noticed how some things come easy? That's because you have God-given natural strengths or talents in those areas. Just concentrate on these strengths. Dig them out of the ground where they've been buried and grow the Tree of Life.

Allow the Lord to bring forth your latent potential and capability into functional ministry. Desire to find the release into your foreordained purpose — to become who you already are inside. Discover your true identity. decide to fulfill it. Determine your priorities. The *desire* to diligently fulfill your prophetic vision will lead you.

What you do with your life is what will happen.

ASPIRE TOWARD YOUR DESIRE:

- Let that desire be exclusively and inexorably linked to the will of the Father.
- Let your goals arise naturally into clear action.
- Enjoy the journey of life toward God's desire.
- See progress in everything you do.

The Happiness of Finding Wisdom

FINDING WISDOM.
Passionate Desire

- Set your own standard and don't be controlled by what others think.
- Prepare for momentum and drive toward success. Work toward desire.
- Prepare to be satisfied with nothing less than the unconditional completion of all God's purposes for your life.

DILIGENCE:

Obtaining happiness requires the reexamination of the basic premises by which you live your life and a starting afresh with clear awareness and decisiveness of where you really should go. You're the steward of your life. Only through great desire will you have the diligence to perform the necessary tasks and overcome adversity.

Adversity causes some men to break -- and others to break records.
William A. Ward

Building with Wisdom takes work. You can't sit around wishing that things would work out. When Elisha asked for a double portion, Elijah replied, **"Thou hast asked a hard thing; nevertheless, if thou see me when I am taken..."** (2 Kings 2:10). Then several times, Elijah tried to trick him into not being around at the right time. Elisha must have felt discouraged. He had to be persistent and work to obtain his objective. When you have a dream, you must be willing to do what it takes to make it happen. Relentless and resolute persistence is the condition to obtaining the dream.

Self-diligence can be defined as making application with a careful degree of effort toward a known objective. It is simply doing what must be done, regardless of whether we feel like doing it or not. It's usually easier to stop thinking about it – and just do it. Even if we "hate" the individual job, we need to diligently stick to our decisions no matter what. Diligence leads to the discovery of new dignity, invigorated creativity, vitality, spontaneity, and ... even some laughter.

Where do we find that elusive key of self-diligence? Poets and philosophers have searched for centuries. But, we need to search no further. The Bible tells us that God has already given us everything that pertains to life and godliness (2 Pet. 1:3). All that's left for us is to see the house we're to become -- unlock our passion — then transform our thinking and manage our lives.

** Write about the issues you now face that require you to have diligence.
** Write about how you can live your life more redemptively.

The Happiness of Finding Wisdom

FINDING WISDOM
Passionate Desire

SOOOO, YOU'RE WAKING UP?

Now that we're wakeful, we wonder where we've been the rest of our lives! Becoming cognizant of our God-given prophetic vision takes us to the exciting discovery of our dramatic God-given desires. Now, only diligently following those desires can begin to break us free from the mental imprisonment of previous lifestyles. Discipleship means being a "diligent or trained one." The Greek word is *matheteuo*; to become a pupil, enroll as scholar, to be instructed and taught. Diligence is the portal into actualizing LIFE. It opens the way to discover this whole possibility of being successful.

Jesus diligently focused Himself toward what needed to be done. Luke 9:51 says that He resolutely set out to go to Jerusalem (NIV), He steadfastly set His face to go (NKJ), He was determined to go (NASU), He moved steadily onward with and iron will (LB), He set His face as a flint on the goal. In like determination, Paul purposed to change the world (Acts 19:21).

The main reason for unhappiness is the trading of what we want (desire) most for what we want right now.

Diligence... it's not a ninety-nine cent item at the fast-food restaurant. I can't grit my teeth and wish that I can have it. No. Godly character doesn't come from a list of things to do. It's not accomplished by will power. It's no longer just hearing and doing that matters. To the NEW CREATION, what matters is BEING. And that means slowly becoming more like Him.

- Diligence comes by experience.
- Diligence requires sustained daily effort.
- Moving toward God's directive is the ultimate factor in determining success.

YOUR GODLY VISION CAUSES WISE DECISIONS:

The unrenewed nature wrestles against this vision, trying to perpetuate an internal struggle between your wants and God's plan. It tries to draw you back into sorrow. But, each time you diligently choose to break free from the power of your already dead "old man," you move toward your prophetic vision. Today, you can begin to purposefully disengage from that old life — like an infant from the umbilical, like the space shuttle from its booster. Each day as you move towards God's plan, you become more whole. It's conscious living.

FINDING WISDOM
Passionate Desire

Vision reveals the God-given blueprint for our building. If we don't have a vision – then we won't have a well-built life. God-given prophetic vision enables every decision. When we face a dilemma of what to do next, we must remember that our decisions create our future reality.

Wisdom = The ability to acquire vision, to decide correctly and then follow the best course of action.

There are times when we just don't know what to do. Maybe we're just confused. A lot of us avoid making a decision, for fear of making the wrong one. That's when we need to remember that God can take even our worst mistakes and somehow work it for our good.

There are times when some decisions seem urgent. We exist in a world that coerces us to conform and to perform urgently. Distractions are always present -- and they're never passive. They often come to coax us into double-mindedness. Our choices can build us or to bind us. We must discern each possibility. That's why we spell success: M.a.k.i.n.g. G.o.o.d. D.e.c.i.s.i.o.n.s.

Remember that we are the product of our decisions. Every decision moves us in the direction of our future.

Not making the right decisions could limit our lives! We should watch out for unexpected choices that could change the course of our lives: Samson lost sight of his overall game plan by allowing Delilah to bring him to his limits. Esther, on the other hand, made the choice to endanger her position of royalty in order to fulfill her purpose and save her people. Baby Moses floated down the bulrushes in the little basket – lost until the Pharaoh's daughter *decided t*o rescue him. Rahab *decided* to lie and saved the spies. Then there were people like Simeon & Anna who *chose* to reach beyond the confined limits of their lives into the place of their destiny and purpose.

Jesus arrived at this place of decision. He told Pontius Pilate, "Toward this end, I was born." He knew the plan for His life and died to keep it. Jesus continued to give us the example, "I must be about my Father's business." Gethsemane was a decision. We can choose the mundane or to obtain the Pearl of Great Price. We must seek the kingdom. Using wisdom to make correct choices and detail our lives is a sacred obligation.

You haven't been this way before (Josh.3:4).

Actualizing dreams depends on the ability to perceive those special *kairos* moments and then make correct decisions. *Kairos* times are highly charged with urgency to break into

FINDING WISDOM
Passionate Desire

uncharted realms and to cooperate with the global plan for this earth. We must discern that call to significance and proceed with clarity. It's the "new thing" (Is. 42:9).

Still, there are non-negotiable assignment that we must do them. 1 Thessalonians 5:16-23 commands us to rejoice evermore. Pray without ceasing. In everything give thanks. Quench not the Spirit. Despise not prophesying. Prove all things. Hold fast to good.

WISDOM LEADS TO CORRECT DECISIONS IN THESE AREAS OF LIFE (PROVERBS):

Being rightly related to God.
Moral excellence.
Diligence (10:4-5).
Food (12:11, 20:13, 27:18, 28:19)
Sobriety (20:1, 23:20).
Responsibility (12:24).
Self-satisfaction (24:4).
Ease (15:19).
Honor (22:29).
Wealth and life (33:4).
Grace (3:34).
Being "lowly in spirit" (16:19).
Patience and self-control (14:29, 17:27, 19:11, 29:11).
Settles quarrels (15:18).
Courage (28:1),
Love (10:12, 6:6).
Truthfulness (12:17, 19, 22, 14:5).
Kindness (11:17).
Kindness to animals (12:10)
Kindness to poor and needy (14:21, 31, 19:17).
Generosity (11:25, 22:9).
Honesty as a witness in court (12:17).
Honesty in business transactions (11:1, 16:11).
Teachableness (10:8, 12:1, 13:1, 13, 18, 15:5).
Using correct words in restraint (10:19, 11:12, 13:3, 15:28).[1]

---

1. Zuck, Roy B., *"Learning from the Sages"* Baker Books 1995 pg. 105

FINDING WISDOM.
Passionate Desire

MAKING WISE DECISIONS CHANGES WHAT NEEDS TO BE CHANGED.

Being wise means that you build the house and become all that God intended. Every quality in His Name is yours: abundance, excellent overcoming, provision, health, and protection. Discipleship (obtaining image and likeness) establishes you in readiness and priority positioning. Just stretch out and run to obtain the prize of the high calling – it's just ahead.

**Review outloud your hidden dreams. Remember the little anecdotal example about the violinist who could play exquisite music only when the violin strings were tuned in proper tension daily. In that comparison, we can only grow when extended beyond what we are today to whom we can be tomorrow.

While trying to become diligent and make wise decisions, we need to just mention some of the down sides that you may not be prepared to face unless you know about them.

- <u>Discouragement</u>. Progress may be slower than you expect. Continue at a comfortable pace knowing that real changes occur only at their own speed; this speed might seem quick on some days, and slow on others. A gentler pace gives the time to reinforce new habits through repetition.

- <u>Impatience</u>. Be willing to try many different approaches. Because we're different types of people with different goals, a single technique won't work for everybody. There's no "pat answer."

- <u>Ineffectiveness</u>. Express your new resolves by acting "as if" they are true; behave as if you were the person you want to be with the behavior and thoughts that you desire. If the new "you" is based on a reexamination of your God-given vision, then this "acting out" is based on neither falsehood nor superficial manipulation — it becomes the honest behavior of the new you. Eventually, the new script becomes incorporated into your personality, and it is now "who you really are."

Beware of the possible downside to making changes. There may be obstacles such as:

- When we change, we're no longer who we were. There may be feelings of emptiness as we lose the perceived benefits from undesirable behaviors.

- <u>An obsession with the self</u>. Sometimes, excessive introspection may divert us from our path of selflessness. We can become introverted and neglectful of our dealings with everyday life.

The Happiness of Finding Wisdom

FINDING WISDOM
Passionate Desire

- <u>The burden of the responsibility.</u> Sometimes we might feel that change becomes a treadmill requiring constant effort. At those times, we can slack off and take a day to relax.
- <u>Relapses</u>. They might indicate that the chosen goal wasn't right for us. Some relapses can be disregarded as a part of the natural ups-and-downs of the growth process, but relapses require close inspection.
- <u>Alienation of friends and family</u>. Although we are becoming a "better" person, some people might be uneasy.
- <u>Idealism</u>. Progress doesn't necessarily mean that we'll conquer all of our problems; it means going from one group of difficulties to another.
- <u>A worsening of conditions</u>. Sometimes, moving forward makes circumstances temporarily worse and not better.

WE BUILD AND CONSTRUCT OUR LIVES BY CHANGING INTO WISDOM.

- Find the purpose of God. Build the structure that incorporates wisdom.
- Possess the desire to change toward that purpose — the door to a new house. In order to change on the outside, we must change on the inside.
- Decide to give your attention to this desire to change. Set your will upon this desire. (Is. 1:19). Mortify your own desires. "Thy will be done."
- Learn to make diligent, voluntary, and purposeful transformation.
- Participate in the *Awesome* Reverence of God.
- Deepen your *knowledge* base; obtain the information needed to change.
- Let *understanding* be the mirror to your change. See yourself putting action upon your desire — allow your life to reflect the will of God.

Transformation comes by a righteous resolve, and God induced effort to change; it is not the work of human flesh. This yields a great to <u>desire</u> to apprehend the Wisdom of God.

Wisdom will build the house of God.

Whatever you do, work at it with all your heart, as working for the Lord.
(Col. 3:23 NIV)

The Happiness of Finding Wisdom

WISDOM BUILDS THE HOUSE

LADY WISDOM:

Wisdom = the conviction of a fixed upright order to which wise people submit their life.

Throughout this book, we'll study how the Proverb's lady named Wisdom built her house. We'll find that our Wise woman *desired* to fulfill her destiny. Therefore, she has something to say and she goes out to where the people are. Her *passionate desire* propels her earnest message. Her lifestyle extends her message (diligent discipleship). She intends to enlighten others – that's her *purpose*.

> Wisdom is always described as a woman. The Bible is filled with profound examples of wise women who touched the world in powerful and meaningful ways. It was Solomon's way of describing the qualities incorporated in that concept. So, don't be put off about this being a story about a woman -- by now, most of us know that the church is described as a woman, so we all have to learn to become that virtuous bride who embodies the attributes of wisdom.

Solomon tells us to love this woman called "Wisdom." After all, (Prov. 4:6) he knew about all kinds of women, but only found one. Wisdom is the one *virtuous* woman depicted in Proverbs 31. She perceived what needed to be accomplished (the plan) and did it with fervor. It wasn't with *virtue* like we think of today as chastity and innocence. No. Two hundred times the Hebrew Bible translates *cha-yil* as "force or ability," but only in this instance is it translated "virtue or chastity." (Strongs #ity, *cha-yil,* means might, strength, power, able, valiant, valor, riches, substance, and wealth).[1] *Cha-yil* means to be a potent powerful force that accomplishes tasks.

31:11, She did not make foolish decisions.
31:16, She used discretion and didn't make hasty choices.
31:18, She was wise in business dealings.
31:26, She used thoughtful words and didn't speak without thinking.
31:28, Her home was harmonious with healthy relationships.

---

1. Zodhiates, Spiros, "*The Hebrew-Greek Key Study Bible, Lexical Aids to the Old Testament,*" (Baker Book House, 1985).

WISDOM BUILDS THE HOUSE
Lady Wisdom:

Let's interpret this Proverb again with new understanding. This valiant, watchful, and alert wife never sat idle (v27). She <u>built</u> because she was enlightened to know and understand (had revelation of) her "strength, force and ability" in God. That's why her husband trusted her. And God will trust you.

WHAT THIS PROVERBS WOMAN DOES (1:20-23)
Wisdom crieth (shouts with joy earnestly to be heard)
Without; she uttereth her voice in the streets (open broad places):
She crieth in the chief place of concourse (a place of "rat-race," or "at noisy intersections" – Berkeley)
In the openings (entrances)
Of the gates (she speaks to important people about important subjects):
In the city she uttereth her words. Wisdom is not confined to her home or her church, she goes into the city market places and through the arenas of government. She doesn't hide from the real world, nor does she become tainted by it.

WHAT WISDOM SAYS:
How long, ye simple (foolish, silly, stupid, or carnal)
Ones, will ye love simplicity? And the scorers (those of derision)
Delight in their (emphatic) **scorning, and fools** (fat or stupid ones)
Hate knowledge (being aware)? She sure doesn't beat around the bush, but is direct, knowing that change will enable greatness. Look at the following promise.
Turn you at my reproof: behold, I will pour out my spirit unto you,
I will make known my words unto you. (KJV) Wisdom calls the simple to repentance and then promises to fill them with God's spirit. That will allow them to "know" the words that she speaks are true.

> *Wisdom, like an inheritance, is a good thing and benefits those who see the sun.*
> *Wisdom is a shelter as money is a shelter, but the advantage of knowledge is this:*
> *that wisdom preserves the life of its possessor.*
> Eccl. 7:11-12 NIV

ADVANTAGES & ATTRIBUTES OF WISDOM.
- In wisdom, God made all earth's creatures (Ps. 104:24-26).
- The wise listen and add to their learning (Prov. 1:2-7).
- Wisdom will save you from the ways of wicked men, (Prov. 2:12)

The Happiness of Finding Wisdom

WISDOM BUILDS THE HOUSE.
Lady Wisdom:

- It will save you also from the adulteress, from the wayward wife. (2: 16 NIV)
- Wisdom adds years to your life (Prov. 3:16).
- Wisdom could be passed from person to person. Moses laid hands on Joshua, who was then filled with the spirit of wisdom (Deut. 34:9).
- It leads you along straight paths (Prov. 4:11).
- When you walk, your steps will not be hampered (Prov. 4:12).
- You must turn your ear to wisdom (Prov 2:2).
- When you run, you will not stumble (Prov. 4:10-.12).
- Wisdom allows you to maintain discretion and your lips preserve knowledge (Prov. 15:7).
- Wisdom is found on the lips of the discerning (Prov 10:13).
- Wise men store up knowledge (Prov. 10:14).
- A man is praised according to his wisdom (Prov. 12:8).
- Wisdom reposes in the heart of the discerning (Prov 14:33).
- Wisdom is better to get than gold (Prov 16:16).
- Wisdom is found in those who take advice (Prov. 13:10).
- With humility comes wisdom (Prov 11:2).
- The wisdom of the prudent is to give thought to their ways... (Prov 14:8)
- The wise show restraint (Prov 23:4).
- A wise man has great power (Prov 24:5-6).
- Wisdom is sweet to the soul; if you find it, there is a future hope for you,
- And he who walks in wisdom is kept safe (Prov 24:14).
- A man who loves wisdom brings joy to his father (Prov 29:3).
- The rod of correction imparts wisdom (Prov 29:15).
- A wise wife speaks with wisdom and faithful instruction (Prov. 31:26).
- The wise man has eyes in his head (Eccl. 2:14).

The Happiness of Finding Wisdom

WISDOM BUILDS THE HOUSE
Lady Wisdom:

- God endows the heart with wisdom and gives understanding to the mind (Job 38:36-37).
- Wisdom is found among the aged (Job 12:12).
- One wise man is more powerful than ten rulers in a city (Eccl. 7:19).
- A poor wise man delivered the city by his wisdom (Eccl. 9:14-15).
- Wisdom is better than weapons of war (Eccl. 9:18).
- Wisdom brightens a man's face and changes its appearance (Eccl. 8:1).
- A discerning man keeps wisdom in view... (Prov 17:24).
- The fountain of wisdom is a bubbling brook (Prov 18:4).
- He who gets wisdom loves his own soul (Prov 19:8).
- Wisdom comes from God to administer justice (1 Kings 3:28).
- Wisdom gives patience to overlook an offense (Prov 19:11 NIV).

THE TWO SIDES OF WISDOM:

Zophar claimed that Job just wanted to hear himself talk and that he was a mocker. However, in this unfortunate dialogue, we learn a very important truth about wisdom. Job 11:5-6, **Oh, how I wish that God would speak, that he would open his lips against you and disclose to you the secrets of wisdom, <u>for true wisdom has two sides</u>.** NIV

> Barnes Notes talks about this thought of the two sides of wisdom: "Of the words used in the Hebrew, the sense of two sides is not difficult. The word *kiplayim*, "double," ... means a doubling... that of two folds, or double folds, and the sense here is that the wisdom of God is ... complicated, inexplicable, or manifold. It is not spread out and plain, but is enfolded, so that it requires to be unrolled to be understood... Hence, it means that the wisdom of God is... so enfolded, so complex, that it greatly surpasses our comprehension."[1]

We only see a small part of the "secrets" of His wisdom — the remainder of His wisdom (still unfolded), is far above our current grasp. Only a very small part is unrolled so that we can read it. When will we peer into that which remains unopened? When will we pen-

---

1. From Barnes' Notes, Electronic Database. Copyright (c) 1997 by Biblesoft.

The Happiness of Finding Wisdom

etrate the involutions, so as to perceive and understand it? Yes, it is reserved for us to discover throughout our life in the eternal now.

THE OTHER FACETS OF WISDOM:

As our thinking changes, then our soul heals and our spirit deepens. We live by every Word of God (Matt. 4:4) and are able to reproduce it. Luke 21:15, **For I will give you a mouth** (to declare) **and wisdom** *(sophia, insight into the true nature of things),* **which all your adversaries shall not be able to gainsay nor resist.** (KJV) Nothing can resist!

1 Cor 12:8, **For to one is given by the Spirit the word** *(logos)* **of wisdom...** (KJV)

Job 28:12-19, **But where can wisdom** *(Chokmah,* the ability to make the right choices at the opportune time.) **be found?... Man does not comprehend its worth; it cannot be found in the land of the living. The deep says, `It is not in me'; the sea says, `It is not with me.' It cannot be bought with the finest gold, nor can its price be weighed in silver...the price of wisdom is beyond rubies...**

20-23 Where then does wisdom come from? It is hidden from the eyes of every living thing, concealed even from the birds of the air. God understands the way to it and he alone knows where it dwells ...When he... made a decree for the rain and a path for the thunderstorm, then he looked at wisdom and appraised it; he confirmed it and tested it (NIV).

Proverbs 9:12 sums it up, **"If you are wise, you are wise for yourself, and if you scoff, you will bear it alone."** If you... you... alone. This shows that you control the choice of your own fate.

THE GIFT

King Solomon was called the wisest man and he used that wisdom to construct God's house. Let's examine further characteristics of Solomon's wisdom. 1 Kings 3:9 tells us that Solomon could discern between good and evil. 1 Kings 4:29-31 says, **God "gave" Solomon wisdom and very great insight, and a breadth of understanding as measureless as the sand on the seashore.** Solomon's wisdom was greater than the wisdom of all the men of the East, and greater than all the wisdom of Egypt (type of worldly wisdom 1 Kings 10:24). The whole world sought audience with Solomon to hear the wisdom God had put in his heart. NIV This Godly wisdom didn't come naturally; it was a *gift* (2 Kings 4:33). Wisdom is in the deepest sense a divine gift (see Acts 6:10; 1 Cor 2:6; 12:8; Eph 1:17; Col 1:9; 3:16; James 1:5; 3:15-17

The Happiness of Finding Wisdom

WISDOM BUILDS THE HOUSE
Lady Wisdom:

The Queen of Sheba (whose name meant seven, fullness, and completeness) recognized this wisdom by *seven* OBSERVABLE ACCOMPLISHMENTS: she saw (1 Kings 10:4-5) the temple, the food on his table, his servants, the attendants, the waiters and how they were dressed, his cupbearers, and his entry way. The gift of Wisdom allowed Solomon to display a competent lifestyle.

But, what a paradox — the wisest man ended his life unwisely! At least by the end of his life, he did recognize his foolishness. Solomon's life illustrates that "once wise" doesn't mean "always wise." Like the rest of us, Solomon was influenced by his passive decisions, peer pressure, and external social expectations (Ecc. 11:9).

To understand God's wisdom, we must examine the "should have been" strength of Solomon as a king. We can learn how to properly use this wisdom for ourselves and not make the same mistakes. This passionate desire to operate in the force of accurate wisdom and to correctly rule the government of God brings to pass the new-dimensional revelation that greatly impacts our cities and nations.

BUILDING OUR "SURE HOUSE."

If what he has built survives, he will receive his reward.
1 Cor 3:14 NIV

As we compare building our life to building a house, the Scriptures tell us about other people who "should have made it." There was an ancient priest named Eli who failed to teach his sons properly. The sons lived an ungodly life and Eli didn't do anything about it. Therefore, God raised-up another leader who would replace Eli (1 Samuel 2:35), **And I will raise me up a faithful priest, who shall do according to that which is in my heart and in my mind: and I will build him a SURE HOUSE; and he shall walk before my anointed forever.**

This same terminology is used again about Jeroboam (1 Kings 11:38), 1 Kings 11:38 ... **If thou wilt hearken unto all that I command thee, and wilt walk in my ways, and do that is right in my sight, to keep my statutes and my commandments. I will be with thee, and build thee a SURE HOUSE...** (KJV). There are four issues to notice on both these verses about the sure house.

The sure house is also translated **"a dynasty as <u>enduring</u> as the one I built for David"** (NIV). A sure house is one that can stand the test of time. That means that our lives don't regress into sloppy or undisciplined ones. We need to focus on endurance and the long haul -- so that our house will withstand the storms and not collapse to temptation. A sure

WISDOM BUILDS THE HOUSE.
Lady Wisdom:

house will stand up under pressure and chastening. Notice also that in each example, the building of this sure house is predicated on <u>obedience</u>. It's not enough to be willing, or to have good intentions, or to want to have a house.

We must build a life of obedience and not self-seeking.

When Joshua was one hundred years old he said, **As for me and my house, we will serve the Lord.** His "house" represented the various components of his life. The "me" and the "my" of this statement not only represent his family but his own body and soul coming into line with his spiritual decision.

God builds the house and we help. Psalm 127:1 confirms it, **Except the Lord build the house, they labor** (to burdensomely toil and labor severely without joy) **in vain that build it.** The believer must labor with God in obedience. We understand that becoming a "sure house" means that we BECOME what is in God's heart and mind.

GUARDING YOUR HOUSE MOVES YOU TO NEW DIMENSIONS:

The first Passover (a picture of our salvation) illustrates the critical urgency demanded of the believer to <u>guard</u> his own <u>house</u>. (Exodus 12:17-51). This intense personal preparation is the ultimate requirement before transitioning to the next dimension. As we study this famous feast, let's consider how it applies to our living a life of wisdom.

- No uncircumcised person was allowed to participate (43-51).

- On the first day of the first month of the year, (Nissan — our March/April), leaven (that which spreads rapidly) was to be removed from the whole house. Removal of leaven represents a type of separation from sin. Characteristics of internal defilement and old patterns that could grow were to be purged from each house (see 1 Cor. 5:6-8).

- A holy convocation was called and no one could stand "afar off" (Ex. 12:16).

- Each household must participate in the experience for themselves, but they could share the Lamb with their neighbor if needed.

- The sacrificial lamb (for each house) was killed (1 Pet. 1:19-20) at twilight by the whole assembly in a spirit of oneness (we all killed Him). This entire sacrifice implies multiple sacrifices counted as one corporate Sacrifice by God.

- The unblemished lamb (Ex. 12:5, 1 Pet. 1:19) was killed (Ex. 12:6, John 12:24, 27), roasted in the fire with unleavened bread (type of sanctified

The Happiness of Finding Wisdom

WISDOM BUILDS THE HOUSE
Lady Wisdom:

walk and conversation (Mark 8:15, Gal. 5:9), and bitter herbs (which represent repentance (2 Cor. 2:15-17).

- The Israelites were to be fully dressed and ready to go (vs. 11, see Eph. 6:14, Heb. 12:2). Their shoes were to be on their feet (ready to run — see also Acts 7:33, 13:25). The staff was to be in their hand (ready to run farther – Ps. 23:4, Zech. 8:4, Heb. 11:21).

- The lamb was to be eaten in haste (acted out in faith—ready to leave any moment).

- Apparently the lamb was slain at the threshold or doorway of the house. Hyssop dipped in blood must then cover the lintel and two doorposts (prefiguring blood at His head, hands and feet) at the door (of our temple —heart Ex. 12:7, Heb. 9:22) so that the Lord would "pass over" (meaning hop, skip, dance, leap) and not allow the destroyer to come into the house. Only the blood made the immunity difference between the Israelite and Egyptian households.

- Israel's actions speak of our needed behavior modifications in order for protection and survival during crisis. "Now the blood shall be a sign on your house" (vs. 13).

- This would be a night of awakened vigil with thanksgiving to the LORD for bringing them out of Egypt (vs. 42). All past subjugation, philosophical supposition, heritage, custom, tradition, and blinding mentalities must be put aside – leaving them vigilant for the final dispatchment assignments of the Lord.

- They were to stay in the house until daybreak (under protection provided in their dwelling place with God). Observance of these expectations was a matter of life and death.

- "On that very same day" that Israel went forth from Egypt" – the new order broke free and began great exploits.

- A memorial (remembrance, celebration) of Passover was to be kept forever (vs. 14). Jesus became the Passover Lamb for our house which we celebrate with the Lord's Supper (Matt. 27:17-30, Mark 14:12-26, John 13:1-30 etc.).[1] As we obey and respond in faith, we move to new dimensions.

---

1. Varner, Kelly, Book on Exodus, Self-published.

The Happiness of Finding Wisdom

WISDOM BUILDS THE HOUSE.
Lady Wisdom:

FURTHER DIMENSIONS:

Many of our Bible heros discovered invisible dimensions of God. Enoch walked with God and was not. (Gen. 5:24). Because Moses was overly concerned about people's problems, he saw that new dimension, but was unable to access it. But, it's how God sent a ram into the thicket before Abraham climbed the mountain with Isaac. It's why David dared to eat the priest's bread and found the very heart of God. These "new places" are unexplored territories that transcend the present known structure of things. Jesus lived in them... He walked on water. That's how He multiplied loaves and fishes. God said He would make known the end from the beginning.

> *Praise be to...God ... wisdom and power are His. He ...gives wisdom to the wise and knowledge to the discerning. He reveals deep and hidden things.*
> Dan. 2: 20-23

Having God's wisdom unveils mysterious hidden concepts that no one has thoroughly searched out. They are there, you know. It's easier to imagine these hidden dimensions when we remember that we hear only a small section of the sound waves. Dogs hear higher frequencies than we can detect. Porpoise and dolphins communicate in levels beyond our ability to discern. Elephants communicate on lower levels than we can hear. But it's all there the whole time. We see only a small part of the light wave. This isn't a fairyland delusion. In the same way, there are unsearched dimensions in the spirit, just waiting for us to heed – to plug into the frequency and hear a new sound– to perceive dimensional insight – to apprehend new arenas of understanding.

We must transition with God into new dimensions. We must discern where the cloud moves, and obediently follow it. Old ways must give way to new ways. Old information must be replaced by relevant proceeding insight. Transitioning must be planned movement in a forward, proceeding direction (Josh. 4:3-9).

THE WISE WIFE BUILDS HER HOUSE:

Lady Wisdom knew how to access "new dimensions." The first thing to notice is that she purposefully "built." And, you must build. No one can do it for you. Prov. 9:1 **Wisdom, She BUILDS.** Jesus said, "I will BUILD my church."

In the New Testament, the word "edification" means to BUILD an edifice or building, (Rom. 15:2, 1 Cor. 14:5, 12, 26, 2 Cor. 10:8, 12:19, 13:10, Eph. 2:21, 4:12, 4:29, 1 Tim. 1:4, etc.). 1 Cor 14:12 NIV- **Even so you, since you are zealous for spiritual gifts, let it be for the edification** (building up) **of the church that you seek to excel.**

The Happiness of Finding Wisdom

WISDOM BUILDS THE HOUSE
Lady Wisdom:

Jesus spoke about the wise man who built his house upon a rock (Matt. 7:24-27). If you build upon the rock of Jesus Christ, then your house can be that "sure house." We must build wisely. Please read along in your Bible as we examine our primary text for this book, Proverbs 9:1. We'll return to this scripture verse many times.

Wisdom (plural as in 1:20 –*Chokmah*, the knowledge and the ability to make the right choices at the opportune time.)
h<u>**as built her house**</u> (already built a permanent dwelling place for God)**.**
She has hewn out her seven (fullness of golden candlesticks, seven horns of power, the seven eyes of revelation, seven rainbow colors, seven colors on Joseph's coat) **pillars;**
She has slaughtered her meat, (she works).
She has mixed (mingled or mixed with honey and spices) **her wine,**
She has also furnished her table (prepared a feast).
She has her maidens, (those others who help).
She cries out from the highest places of the city (she preaches).

Our Lady Wisdom shows us how to build the house that God wants. We'll continue to learn about that house and its pillars, but for now, we need to realize that her construction demands that she follow a floor plan — one board at a time – precept by precept. How ridiculous it would be for her to just gather up a bunch of wood, hay, and stubble and start nailing. We must understand that our prophetic vision (our floor plan) is summed up in the will of God.

CHOOSING TO USE THE BLUEPRINT:
Jeremiah 29:11-12 says that God has a detailed plan for our lives, **For I know the plans I have for you… plans to prosper you and not to harm you, plans to give you hope and a future** (NIV).

We'll call this plan the blueprint, or floor plan. This original blueprint produces a diagram that utilizes your potential (talents). The Great Architect drafts the overall picture and decides if your house is a skyscraper or a log cabin. He decides the room's dimensions and locates them where He wants them, including the non-external necessities such as the electrical and plumbing plans.

Jesus looks back from the finished work. From our beginning, the Master Builder decrees the present tense of our end result. We must contend earnestly for the faith to comprehend this PROCEEDING Word of God that activates our future... He knows us before we're born. That means that He visualizes our building before we can comprehend it. Or to say it another way, in His mind, there's conception that precedes our under-

The Happiness of Finding Wisdom

WISDOM BUILDS THE HOUSE.
Lady Wisdom:

standing. He does that so that we would have to seek Him for the plan of action with which to structure and build our lives. Out from the Father's heart, our mission unfolds – there's a foundation [30 fold], structure [60 fold], and a completion [100 fold] of our building project. That's Christ abiding within our temple. Every project should progress toward that desired end.

Our job is to DISCERN that plan and then decide to create this one wonderful design. The builder (us) builds what the Architect designs.

THAT HOUSE:

There are many metaphors about us being the house or the temple of God. Moses diligently followed the pattern to build and carry the dwelling place of God – His tabernacle. According to the Jewish Talmudists, the Tabernacle was to be an insight into deeper wisdom, something more splendid than itself. It was to shadow heavenly and eternal things. Moses was instructed to put the two stone tablets of God's Word in the ark of the tabernacle (typifying how we put the Word in us). By means of this Tabernacle, God attempted to convey truths of reality and certainty to His people. It was through this similitude that we find a "shadow of the good things to come" (Heb. 8:1,2,4,5, 10:1). The Tabernacle contained the foundation of God's entire plan for our world – every detail, every color, every piece of material; number, dimension, position, and article of furniture spoke of special significance.

Fifty chapters of God's Word describe this portable house (Ex. = 13 chapters; Lev. =18 chapters; Numb. =13 chapters; Deut. =2 chapters; Heb. = 4 chapters; plus many other references). God considers His house to be of great importance. The great song sung in the courts of heaven (Revelation 15:3) tells about His house. This theme of God's house presents a pattern that's consistent throughout Scripture.

It was King David who received the plan for the temple. David had it in his heart to build a house of rest for the ark and for the footstool of God (1 Chron. 28:2). But, his lifestyle of war kept him from building. He gave his son Solomon the detailed instructions to build God's house. Solomon actually constructed the plan. Solomon spent seven years building God's house - - it became one of the seven wonders of the ancient world. Then, he spent thirteen more years building an even grander house for himself! Unfortunately, Solomon became more concerned with building a house (name) for himself than a house for God. Soon the nation divided in civil unrest.

Now, we're told to build a house for God, not ourselves. Jesus is the chief cornerstone. Our new man is the house with new walls. Our walls are salvation (Is. 26:1, 60:18). Isaiah also points out that our walls are continually before the Lord (49:16). Zech 2:5 says

The Happiness of Finding Wisdom

WISDOM BUILDS THE HOUSE
Lady Wisdom:

that God will be a wall of fire and He will be its glory within. Our salvation stands to protect the fiery presence of God inside and it contains the structure of the New Creation.

2 Corinthians 5:17 says, **If any man be in Christ, then he has become a NEW CREATION.** The Greek word for <u>new creation</u> is *ktisis* which is sometimes translated "building or architect." We become a new building! *Katoika* means residence or habitation. *Katoiketerion* means dwelling pace or abode. *Katoikesis* means residence or mansion and *Katoikeo* means to house permanently or reside. Note these Scriptural examples:

- Acts 7:48 – "The most High DWELLETH not in temples made with hands"
- Acts 17:24 – "God…DWELLETH not in temples made with hands"
- Acts 17:26 – "Of one blood all nations of men for to DWELL on…the earth"
- Eph. 2:22 – "Are builded together for an HABITATION of God through the Spirit"
- Eph. 3:17 – "That Christ may DWELL in your hearts by faith"
- Col. 1:19 – "For it pleased the Father that in Him should all fullness DWELL"
- Col. 2:9 – "For in him DWELLETH all the fullness of the Godhead bodily"
- 2 Pet. 3:12 "New heavens…wherein DWELLETH righteousness.[1]

Micah 7:11 states, **In the day when your walls are to be built, in that day your boundaries shall be extended** (RAMV). You can be sure, God's teaching us to build His house in ourselves. The related concepts of our building and then God extending our building's dimensions are connected. Yes, today is the day to build. This is the hour for aggressively transforming our character into an established maturity. It's time to achieve dimension and expansion; it's time to demonstrate God's grandeur across this world (Ecc. 3:11).

- **The Lord <u>is in</u>** (abides in) **this holy temple** (Ps. 11). Once we build our house, God abides.

---

1. Varner, Kelly, Newsletter Aug. 2000

The Happiness of Finding Wisdom

WISDOM BUILDS THE HOUSE.
Lady Wisdom:

THE BOUNDARIES OF THE HOUSE

The dimensions (size, shape, structure) of our house are God given (Gen. 6:14-16, Ez. 40, 41, Hab. 36, Rev. 21:16-17). We can look at Noah's Ark for our example. It was 300 cubits in length (Gen:14-16). The word for "length" in Hebrew is *orek* which means "forever." The length of God's house stretches throughout eternity and lives forever. 300 represents total redemption (Gen. 52:22) and victory (Judges 7:16, 2 Sam. 23:18).

The breadth (width) of Noah's house was 50 cubits. The word "breadth" means to broaden, enlarge, and to make room. Here we see a concept of giving breadth and expansion to God's presence in our lives (Is. 54:2). We become enlarged to make room for His glory! Our house contains His abiding! (Of course, fifty represents Pentecost and liberty/Jubilee. At Pentecost we receive His power to become enlarged into the formation of His image.) The height of Noah's Ark was 30 cubits. Thirty represents maturity, completion, and consecration. God longs for us to grow into the full stature of the pattern Son, (Eph. 4:13).

Each of us become a sanctuary, the dwelling place of God built in accordance with the pattern revealed (Ex. 25:9). We frail (earthen/human) vessels possess the precious treasure of the grandeur and exceeding greatness of His power (2 Cor. 4:6-7 AMP). We contain His name, His nature, His likeness and image.[1]

In Isaiah, the Lord asks, "Where is the house that you will build Me?" Oh what a question for believers in the last days – we are so busy being busy. And God continues, "Where is the place of My rest?" (Is. 66:1) The Lord yearns to birth a new paradigm – an abiding place of His rest…. In me — in you – and in those who embrace His word.

Rest is not inactivity, but the ceasing from our own works (plans & schemes) and entering into His work.

WE ARE HIS BUILDING

Each individual house becomes fitly framed (Eph. 2:21) --and fitly joined one to another (4:13) in order to become the total habitation of God -- the measure (metron or limited portion) of the stature (as big as) the fullness (completion) of Christ. He alone is the measure that determines our boundaries. 1 Cor 3:9, **For we are labourers together with God: ye are God's husbandry** (garden), **ye are God's building** (KJV). The corporate company of believers ("we are") becomes God's garden and His building. Paul then tells believers how to build their lives with what they learned. He describes three types of

---

[1]. Durden, Ken & Pam, "The House of His Glory" Bridal Affections for idea.

The Happiness of Finding Wisdom

WISDOM BUILDS THE HOUSE
Lady Wisdom:

builders: the wise man (vs. 12,14), the unwise (15), and the foolish (vs. 17). The wise work is solid and enduring, the unwise is not lasting, and the foolish work does not belong to God.

Whether we desire a natural or spiritual house, in both cases building must occur. We build our beliefs and value systems -- these color every experience that funnels into our central nervous system. Just like we interpret a game of sports differently depending on which team we support -- we discern opportunity and failure depending on our frame of reference. Our interpretation of circumstances tends to dictate our future ability to make decisions. The problem of instability erodes our structure whenever we build our lives and ministry on false (sandy) foundations.

> 1 Cor 3:10-15, I (Paul) **laid a foundation** (Jesus) **as an expert builder, and someone else is building on it** (that's you and me!). **But each one should be careful how he builds.... If any man builds on this foundation** (Jesus) **using gold, silver, costly stones** (wise building), **wood, hay or straw** (foolish building), **his work will be shown for what it is, because the Day will bring it to light** (or declare and make it plain)... **and the fire will test the quality of each man's work. If what he has built survives, he will receive his reward...** NIV Salvation is a free gift. Rewards are earned or lost. The quality of our choices is the criterion (what sort it is KJV).

NATURAL ELEMENTS BUILD THE NATURAL HOUSES.

WOOD:
> Hag 1:4 **Is it time for you, O ye, to dwell in your cieled** (wood paneled) **houses, and this house lie waste?** (KJV) Scripturally, wood always represents human nature – wood will only build a natural house. For instance, a tradition of a church may require certain dress codes — but that practice produces a "wood builder" lifestyle. If you go along with it, you'll soon LOOK LIKE A MERE "MAN" INSTEAD OF LIKE GOD'S HOLY HOUSE.

HAY:
> Ps 129:6 **Let them be as the grass** (hay) **upon the housetops, which withereth afore it groweth up:**

STUBBLE:
> Exod. 5:12 **So the people were scattered abroad throughout all the land of Egypt to gather stubble instead of straw.**

The Happiness of Finding Wisdom

WISDOM BUILDS THE HOUSE.
Lady Wisdom:

SPIRITUAL ELEMENTS REQUIRED TO BUILD THE SPIRITUAL HOUSE.

GOLD

Gold represents Deity and building with God's authority/ wood is building upon your humanity and authority. Every choice you make is either IN WOOD or IN GOLD.

SILVER

Silver is harder than gold. The trumpets and lampstands in the tabernacle were silver. Silver speaks of living in functional redemption-- while hay speaks of trying to live on the deadness (withered grass) of the word.

PRECIOUS STONES

Speaks of the jewels of priest's chest plate, the believer's crown, and the adornment of the Bride that is valuable and enduring versus stubble that is ultimately worthless.

- Every choice we make is either in the natural (IN ADAM) or IN CHRIST.

- The quality of the construction of our building will be determined by our choices (decisions). Trouble is, it's not always obvious whether we're building with wood, or precious stones! All of us have at one time or another, built out of wrong motives, wrong teachings, or just plain made mistakes! Therefore, in order for our building to turn out correctly, God will BURN UP any effort of ours that can BURN. God seeks HIS building ---THROUGH US. Anything else will be burned up.

BUILDING TO FINISH:

We've been learning about Wisdom's incredible overall plan (2 Tim. 1:9); it is the design of all things – the preparations, controlling factors, and circumstances — that guide us to the perfect will of the Father. This plan was laid out before the beginning of time (2 Tim. 1:9). It is a holy calling — not because of anything we have done but because of "His own purpose and grace" (2 Tim. 1:9).

Prov 24:3 teaches us that…. **Any enterprise is built by wise planning, becomes strong through common sense, and profits wonderfully by keeping abreast of the facts. (TLB)** "Any enterprise," (any project) must be built by wise planning. Wisdom allows you to anticipate and plan for what is needed to <u>finish</u> the project. Jesus becomes the author and finisher of our faith (Heb. 12:2).

The Happiness of Finding Wisdom

WISDOM BUILDS THE HOUSE
Lady Wisdom:

Here again we notice the emphasis upon organizational planning. Perhaps this sounds secular to you – but it's a Bible foundation used from before the onset of time. A plan is made. Luke 14:28 asks which of us intending to build a tower wouldn't sit down first and count how much it will cost and then see if we have enough funds to <u>finish</u> it. Jesus said His food was to do the will of the Father and to <u>finish His work</u> (John 4:34).

Wisdom demands the determination and aptitude to <u>finish</u> the expected plan of God. Wisdom provides the competency to react accurately and effectively in order to accomplish our assignments.

Planning and scheduling helps us value our lifetime – which is holy time. We need to sit down. count the cost, and decide how we'll finish Ask yourself, am I really going to be a full-fledged, whole hogged, never compromising Christian? It won't be easy. It's not enough to just start the job of building your life; you're supposed to finish it. Then others won't say **"This man began to build, and was not able to <u>finish</u>"** (Luke 14:28-30).

Before his death, Paul evaluated his life saying, **"I have fought a good fight** (he kept on going no matter in spite of obstacles), **I have <u>finished</u> my course** (that which was determined for him to accomplish was completed), **I have kept the faith…"** Obviously, this lifestyle required a daily self-denial. But the reward is never-ending.

In His timelessness, God looks back from the end to show us the way toward the goal. He leads us from being "there" already. We don't have to be afraid of the unknown. From the vision of completion we can fashion an effective NOW that continuously unveils the intentions of God and invades our personalized future.

The Holy Spirit comes to lead us to that finished place.

**Write Romans 11:33, 16:25.

WISDOM'S ACTIONS:
                Cries (8:1-3)
                Stands (8:2)
                Calls (8:4)
                Speaks (8:4-9)
                Reproves (8:5)
                Abhors sin (8:7)
                Admonishes (8:10)

The Happiness of Finding Wisdom

WISDOM BUILDS THE HOUSE.
Lady Wisdom:

>   Searches (8:12)
>   Hates (8:13)
>   Counsels (8:14)
>   Advises (8:15)
>   Loves (8:17)
>   Leads (8:20)
>   Blesses (8:21)
>   Rejoices (8:30)
>   Delights (8:31)
>   Builds (9:1)
>   Cooks (9:2)
>   Plans (9:3)
>   Invites (9:5)[1]

HER TWO HANDS

We've been watching Lady Wisdom build a house with the intention to finish it. Now, let's notice what she holds in her hands while she builds. **She (wisdom) is more precious than rubies; nothing you desire can compare with her** (Prov 3:15-16). **Long life is in her right hand; in her left hand are riches and honor** (Prov 3:1-2). Notice that Wisdom has TWO hands. She holds long life in her right hand and in her left are riches and honor Verse 16 repeats the Wisdom's rewards, **My son, do not forget my teaching, but keep my commands in your heart, for they will prolong your life many years and bring you prosperity.** NIV

> Wisdom dwells with prudence, and finds out the knowledge of witty inventions… (Proverbs 8:12).

> Joshua was instructed to turn not to the right hand or the left (Jos. 1:7) – and in like manner, we are not to pursue what she holds in her hands. We seek first the kingdom of God (invisible and intangible wisdom) and then all things (tangible and visible held in the hands) will be apparent (Matt. 6:33).

> Paul speaks of a similar theme when he told Timothy that all men should "raise (both) their hands without wrath (anger) or doubt." (Doubt comes from the pressure of daily life.) Lifting our hands

---

1. Dakes Bible notes

The Happiness of Finding Wisdom

WISDOM BUILDS THE HOUSE
Lady Wisdom:

signifies that we yield ourselves and let go of this present world and it's circumstances. Once we let go of anger and disbelief, then we can hold on to what wisdom holds — long life is in our right hand and in our left is riches and honor.

Again, in 3 John we read, **"Beloved, I wish above all things that thou mayest prosper** (left hand of wisdom) **and be in health** (right hand)..." The balanced contents of wisdom's two hands are our inheritance as we passionately seek Christ, Who is our Wisdom.

GOD WILL SHOW YOU:

God will show you how to build. **"For the Lord giveth wisdom..."** (Prov. 2:6). Paul wrote that God **"Made known to us the mystery of His own will...** (Eph. 1 9). He's gonna' let you know! Understanding that our plan is summed up in Christ, makes this wisdom known to the rulers and authorities in heavenly places. The job of the church is to reveal Christ and His wisdom to the world (Eph. 3:10-12).

Wisdom (the living out of Christ's abiding purpose) is available for you — in this lifetime. It's hidden for you to find. Be assured, you can find God's will for your life. King Solomon said that wisdom was the most important thing — above all, we're to "get it."

Proverbs 4:5 <u>**Get wisdom**</u>.
Proverbs 4:7 **Wisdom is supreme; therefore <u>get wisdom</u>.**
Proverbs 16:16 **How much better to <u>get wisdom</u> than gold...**
Proverbs 23:23 **Buy the truth and do not sell it; <u>get wisdom ...</u>** NIV

** How can you "get wisdom?" Think of one way to do it today.

Inside every believer dwells The Wisdom of the ages. Wisdom manifests itself through proper accomplishments. Wisdom, in the deepest sense, is the divine gift that enables us to practically live and become Christ-like. It means that intelligent and sensible godliness results from properly discerning God's purposes. Wisdom cries out to you again today. When you heed her cry, your life will be changed. If you hear her, she will, **"Speak of excellent things, and the opening of her lips shall be right things"** (Prov. 8:5-6). Let's continue our definition:

Wisdom = the attribute of God that's given to believers to enable them to build.

The Happiness of Finding Wisdom

WISDOM BUILDS THE HOUSE.
Lady Wisdom:

Wisdom = the faculty of our SOUL that fears God, knows God, and understands His will.

HEBREW TERMS FOR WISDOM

1. *Hokma* has the special meaning of "*dexterity, and skill*" in an art (cf. Ex 28:3; 31:6; 36:1-2). It also and more generally means intelligent, sensible, judicious, endued with reason and using it (Deut 4:6; 34:9; Prov 10:1; etc.); skillful to judge (1 Kings 2:9). Thus the Wisdom of Solomon is manifested in his acute judgment (3:26-28; 10:1-8, 5:12; 1:2). Skill in civil matters (Isa. 19:11), interpreting dreams and prophesying (Dan 5:11).

Chockma = the knowledge and the ability to make the right choices at the opportune time. The consistency of making the right choice is an indication of maturity and development. As an attribute of God, wisdom is intimately related to the divine knowledge, manifesting itself in the selection of proper ends with the proper means for their accomplishment. Thus redemption is a manifestation of divine wisdom (Rom 11:33; 1 Cor 1:24; Rev 7:1).[1]

WISDOM EXISTED BEFORE: (PROVERBS 8)

1. God's creations (22).
2. The beginning of this earth (23).
3. The depths and fountains of water (23-24).
4. The mountains and hills (25).
5. The earth, fields, and dirt of the world (26).[2]

Wisdom existed at God's side and watched Him create the world (Prov. 8:27:31). She saw Him separate the waves on the 2nd day and form the land on the 3rd. Wisdom rejoiced at the work that God did (3:19-20). Wisdom knew the objective of this creation was humanity and understood the mediative role between humanity and God. (R.B.Y. Scott suggests 8:20 be translated, "Then I was beside him binding (all) together."[3]

Wisdom brightens (ENLIGHTENS) a man's face and changes its hard appearance.
Eccl. 8:1

---

1. Quote from The New Unger's Bible Dictionary. Originally published by Moody Press of Chicago, Illinois. Copyright (c) 1988.) Eccl 9:13-10:1
2. Dakes Bible, notes
3. Ibid, Zuke, pg. 231, 240.

The Happiness of Finding Wisdom

WISDOM BUILDS THE HOUSE
Lady Wisdom:

THE 1ST STEP—

FEAR

We've talked about what wisdom is; now we'll talk about how to get it. The sturdy foundation of our house allows the storms to beat vehemently and still stand upright (Luke 6:44). Wisdom intends to lay a foundation for an entirely NEW CREATURE – with new modes of thought, new mentalities, and global views.

> **The fear of the LORD is the <u>beginning of wisdom...</u>** Ps. 111:10-112:1 NIV, Prov. 9:10

Fear should be the first revelation of wisdom. Solomon said that to fear God and keep His commandments is the whole (entire) duty of man (Eccl. 12:13). According to this Scripture, fear is the ability to live life with reverence and to be aware of future judgment. Fear is the concrete slab that creates the first step of our building. We can't get to wisdom without beginning in fear — the first step.

FEAR OF THE LORD

> **All the paths of the Lord are mercy and truth unto such as keep His covenant and His testimonies...<u>The secret of the Lord is with them that fear Him;</u> and He will shew them His covenant** (Psa. 25:10, 14).

Just exactly what is the <u>fear of the Lord</u>? Some fittingly say it's the living awareness that God sees everything. <u>This is the *beginning* of wisdom</u>. Fear is where wisdom begins — the first step, the seed. Psalm 147:11 says, **"The Lord takes pleasure in those who <u>fear Him</u>."** Our reward for properly fearing God is that our days become prolonged (Deut. 6:12).

It's not burnt offerings of year old calves that please God, not thousands of rams, not ten thousand rivers of oil, not your firstborn for your transgressions, not the fruit of your body for the sins of your soul. ....Listen! The LORD is calling to the city: to <u>fear his name</u> is wisdom (Mic. 6:9).[1] This word *fear* doesn't mean to cower and be intimidated. It

---

1. Paraphrased for clarity of Mic 6:9 NIV

THE 1ST STEP—
Fear

means to have "awesome reverence," to venerate, respect, adore, and regard as holy — as when Jacob stood in *awe* at the gate of heaven.

The prime enemy of our fulfilled destiny is this lack of Godly fear (lack of reverence).

Lack of "fear" results in disobedience, wavering ignorance, doubt, and impure motives.

> Ps 145:19 **He will fulfill the desire of them that <u>fear</u> him** (KJV).

> Psalms 25:14 pulls us further into desiring this trait. **The secret of the LORD is with them that <u>fear him</u>; and he will shew them his covenant** (KJV).

> Prov 8:13 **If anyone respects and <u>fears</u> God, he will hate evil. For wisdom hates pride, arrogance, corruption, and deceit of every kind** (KJV).

> Prov 14:27 **The <u>fear</u> of the Lord is a fountain of life, to turn one away from the snares of death** (NKJ).

> Prov 15:33-16:1,33 **The <u>fear of the Lord</u> teaches a man wisdom.**

> Psa. 33:5-6 **The LORD … will be the sure foundation for your times, a rich store of salvation and wisdom and knowledge; <u>the fear of the LORD is the key to this treasure</u>.** (NIV)

In the context of the <u>first step of wisdom</u>, James describes this desired reverential behavior like this: (3:17) **But the wisdom that is from above is <u>first pure,</u> then peaceable, gentle, and easy to be entreated, full of mercy and good fruits, without partiality, and without hypocrisy.** (KJV)

The fear of the Lord is the evidence of faith.

A HOUSE BUILT ON FEAR MEANS A HOUSE BUILT ON GODLINESS:
The Old Testament Hebrew word for "fear of the Lord" is the New Testament Greek word *eusibea* which was usually translated Godliness. Getting that concept of *Godliness* demands that we begin to incorporate God's nature into our being. That's sometimes difficult because memories of the OLD MAN work against us-- somehow, we forget redemptive truths. The Adamic nature embraces losing, invites sickness, and allows the enemy to have ground. We gravitate toward mediocrity and live in anxiety -- the OLD

The Happiness of Finding Wisdom

THE 1ST STEP—
Fear

MAN controls us -- until we realize it's DEAD. Only the memories of our old ways hold us back from eternal issues. The carnal nature does not recognize the finished work. My friend, it's over! We're free! Romans 6:6-7 confirms that Old man nature was nailed to the cross and that He who has died (that's me too) is freed from sin. We now can be alive unto God in Christ Jesus!

Paul wrote to Timothy about developing *godliness* (awesome reverence). 1 Tim. 4:1-8:
Now the Spirit (This message is sent to the church in AD 96, consisting of approximately 100,000 members and 12,000 preachers).
Expressly says (Vividly with expression made visible).
That in the latter times (Eventually at the very last of last days)
Some will depart (By a slow withdrawal from basic truth and basic faith {*pistos* truth}
Giving heed (Turning to another direction or another option)
To deceiving spirits (Seducing, taking by the hand and leading off track with familiarity)
And doctrines (Sounds beautiful like truth but keeps us in religious thinking and constant battles with our Old man that's dead).

It's time to step into the reality of Christ IN US. Paul tells Timothy to have nothing to do with godless myths and old wives tales, but rather, **Train yourself to be godly** (4:7). Godliness (awesome reverence) is the new nature that spreads within us as we wisely eat of the Tree of LIFE. Approaching Godly character allows you to build the quality house and live in the "newness of life" (Rom. 6:4). That foundational first step of new life brings eternity into your now.

- The Greek word for LIFE is *Zoe*, (Strongs #2222) defined as life in the "absolute sense as *godliness.*" It means life as God has it, that which the Father has in Himself and which He gave to the Incarnate Son to have in Himself... and that which the Son manifested in the world."

Returning to 1 Tim. 4:8, **"...** But *godliness* (awesome, reverential fear) **is profitable for ALL THINGS, having promise of the life that now is and that which is to come."** Instead of just physical exercise, we train ourselves in godliness. Why? Because it is profitable. Not for a little bit, but for all things. Not just for heaven, but for now too. Everything that tries to take us out of God's character is exercised away – by discipleship. We change what God tells us to change. We begin to partake of the precious promises and be a partaker of the Divine nature. Let's review:

Godly happiness requires finding prophetic revelation (vision).

THE 1ST STEP—
Fear

- Finding prophetic vision releases desire
- Accomplishing desire demands discipleship
- Discipleship advances *godliness and LIFE.*

Godliness (*eusibia*) = The right good reverence toward the Majestic God with an outward action following. Trying to live a pleasing life unto God. Behaving and conforming to God's nature. It is the exercising from within to bring forth the God-like character.

1 Timothy 3:16 says... **"Great is the mystery of *godliness*...** (awesome reverence)." 1 Timothy 6:6-7 says, **"But *godliness* with contentment is great gain. For we brought nothing into this world, and it is certain we can carry nothing out."** We capture *godliness* as a prize. As we change into his likeness, then we begin to overcome. The quality of *godliness* creates the first stair step into our eternal house.

The expression of Godly "fear" is true worship = the conforming into His image.

Ecclesiastes 12:13, **With fear, let us hear the duty of man. Godly reverence and the keeping his commandments are our whole duty.** Fearing God is the action that we take that begins to deliver us from the soulish realm. Soon, we have the ability to make distinction between the spirit and intuition, between anointing and feeling. We practice the presence of God and He lives through every choice we make.

If, as Job said, the thing we FEAR the most will come upon us (Job 3:25) -- then it behove us to FEAR the Lord... and let that awesome reverence come upon us!

** Would people probably call you a "godly person?" Why?

FOOLISH PEOPLE DON'T FEAR:
We've learned how our Proverbs woman of wisdom builds her house. Fools don't fear God -- nor do they build. The Hebrew word for *fool* means to be deceived or seduced (1:10). The fool is easily gullible, stupid, and silly. The fool is naïve (believes everything 14:15), and is willful and irresponsible (1:32). The foolish are empty headed, for they have nothing better to do than chase after vanities (12:11). The fool is quarrelsome (17:28) and knows no restraint (20:3). A fool appears impatient (10:8) and mocks sin therefore, nothing else of worth can be built.

The Happiness of Finding Wisdom

THE 1ST STEP—
Fear

Fools are preoccupied with "bless me" mentalities and self-centered feelings of offence. Fools concentrate on "their needs" and personal benefits alone. They are creatures of undeveloped discernment, shallow desires, and petulant temperaments. Their attitudes make moving forward in the Kingdom impossible.

Fools destroy. **Prov 14:1 Every wise woman buildeth her house: but <u>the foolish plucketh it down</u> with her hands. (KJV)** Fools don't realize that their life is the temple built for God to inhabit (1 Cor. 6:19-20). They don't take charge of building and maintaining this temple – they don't know how the wise are both the carpenter and the janitor of their our own building.

- Did you know that God built the world by wisdom (Prov. 3:19)? Yet, the fool just tears down. A fool impatiently demands his needs be met first. Sometimes, after those needs are met, a fool may even try to meet other's needs. Although somehow, he considers himself superior to others and their less immediate needs. He wants to fulfill the wants of his personality and often allows personal sin to be casual and common.

**<u>Please read chapter 9 of Proverbs</u> in your Bible once again before we continue. You'll need to study each portion of Proverbs 9 that continues the description of the <u>foolish woman</u> (vs.14):

For she <u>sits at the door</u> (sits at the entry of her house, as compared to wisdom who <u>stands</u> at the gate — the ruling place of the city.)
Of her house on a seat <u>by</u> (she sits "nearby" but not quite the right place)
The <u>highest places</u> of the city, (looks like she's a good Christian).
To <u>call</u> (she randomly calls while wisdom urgently cries)
To those who pass by, who go straight on their way (happen to pass by – while wisdom goes where they are):
"Whoever is simple (she calls to people who are stupid and unknowing),
Let him turn in here" (seduction, away from the truth and God's word);
And as for him who lacks understanding, she says to him, "stolen water (a drink taken with no right)
Is sweet, and bread eaten in secret is pleasant." (It will be what you want to hear)
But he does not know that the dead are there (past victims of her lies),
That her guests are in the depths of hell (already dead, but not buried yet). (NKJ)

The Happiness of Finding Wisdom

THE 1ST STEP—
Fear

Notice her voice. Perhaps you've heard that foolish voice that pretends to really care for you. It usually sounds prophetic, "I prayed for hours last night, and I know you should move there, marry me, invest in this deal, etc." Now, look. She thinks she knows it all. Whether or not she does, doesn't matter. For sure you haven't tried her way. Hear what she says. They are the words of far too many Christians these days. She says things like, "do your own thing; find forbidden pleasure; dishonest gain is the best way. Defy God's law. Everything is sweeter if stolen."

Like the spider to the fly, she calls out to the ignorant passerby, implying that sin is fun. She says, "don't live by God's word – it's a dead end road." Or, "You don't need to study, just preach someone else's tape. The stolen word is better anyway." The trap entices people with their own desires. Anyone foolish enough to listen will be destroyed. Her seducing and sidetracking ways are the depths of hell.

This strange woman (false bride) has an identifiable personality — and too many Christians are beginning to act like her. She slyly brings up controversial and confidential matters at inappropriate times. She is religious and influences many to conform to her image and façade rather than the image of Christ. She has a form of Godliness (2 Tim. 3:5) without power. Proverbs 7 tells us more about her – in very firm terms:

> **Hearken unto me now therefore, O ye children, and attend to the words of my mouth. Let not thine heart decline to her ways, go not astray in her paths** (her main purpose is to get you off the mainstream and into compromise).

> **For she hath cast down many wounded: yea, many strong men have been slain by her. Her house is the way to hell, going down to the chambers of death** (NEB He had (woven) wrapped the (funeral) shroud of his boundless folly.

In our carelessness, could we (who were once the dazzling bride of Christ) now have become the foolish woman? Could it be us? The adulterous wife who won't stay home?

You can be certain that God won't abide in foolishness and He won't enter into her house – whether it is that of an individual mentality or a corporate system.

The Happiness of Finding Wisdom

THE 1ST STEP—
Fear

Every wise woman (bride of Christ) **buildeth** (ongoing process) **her house; but the foolish plucketh it down with her hands,** (Prov. 14:1).

- Prov 21:9 **It is better to live in the corner of an attic than with a crabby woman in a lovely home** (TLB).
- Prov 21:19 **It is better to dwell in the wilderness (desert), than with a contentious and an angry woman** (KJV).
- Prov 27:15-16 **A quarrelsome wife is like a constant dripping on a rainy day; restraining her is like restraining the wind or grasping oil with the hand** (NIV).

Read the text Scripture again (Prov. 9) and underline the foolish believer's behavior.

1. Clamorous and without purpose
2. Refuses to plan or build
3. Sits at door. There's just a door but no house! She doesn't build.
4. Sits by the high place. This believer looks like she's in the right place…
5. Calls out. She talks a lot.
6. Gives bad advice.
7. Teaches death - speaks unscriptural words.

Notice that her activities are very religious. She responds with negativity to any situation, regardless of the facts. That negativity also starts with a seed, and progressively grows into a huge tree. Proverbs 1:22 says, **How long, ye simple ones, will ye love simplicity? And the scorners delight in their scorning, and fools hate knowledge.** Who's a fool?

<u>Firstly,</u> a fool has no fear of God. He is concerned with what is his, where he is going, and who he knows.

<u>Secondly,</u> a fool comforts himself in a lifestyle of selfish and frivolous involvements.

<u>Thirdly,</u> a fool disregards pertinent knowledge. He doesn't want to know the truth. He is often dull and heavy hearted not wanting to change his fixed mindsets.

The Happiness of Finding Wisdom

THE 1ST STEP—
Fear

Fourthly, once he hears truth, he refuses to do it. Rebellion becomes the stronghold that causes the fool to react ineffectively. Defiance assaults him with destruction. The fool becomes spiritually weakened when those mandated powers begin to block the light.

And fifthly, the fool talks a lot. Notice how the foolish woman speaks words of disempowerment. Using those foolish words puts our own life on hold. Suddenly – and we don't know exactly how — we don't want to be a Christian anymore, we allow lust to take root and be conceived in our mind, and we become unclean in our thoughts. Maybe we just lose hope, or tell little tiny white lies.

Look at the progression:
- Wrong thoughts =
- Wrong (foolish) words =
- Wrong feelings and emotions =
- Wrong decisions =
- Wrong character =
- Wrong results.

We don't set out to act foolishly, but often we are drawn toward that kind of behavior. Our association with foolishness is compared to adultery. We become intimately involved with partial truths and seducing thoughts that take us off track and kill our ability to complete God's plan.

Because of the identical descriptions, we know that this seductive woman is probably the adulteress that Solomon was so often warned to avoid. Let me paraphrase some of Proverbs:

"Don't turn away from the words of wisdom my son. Love her and she will keep you. Wisdom is the principal thing. Keep her for she is life (Prov. 4). Pay attention my son and keep your heart right. Don't let your foot turn to evil. Watch out how you live and where you go. (Foolishness will ruin everything that you try to build in your life.)

The lips of the immoral woman drip honey, her words sound wonderful and sweet. But in the end she is bitter as wormwood (the same word as Chernobyl, brain worms — a painful death that has no escape. This is also the same word for the illegal drug now commonly called Absinthe). Her feet go down to death and her ways

The Happiness of Finding Wisdom

are unstable. Listen my son. Don't be intimate with things that are not wise. Drink water from your own cistern (a protected storage for water that is privately owned) and let the running water be your own well (only be intimate with that which is rightful and true). Why should an immoral woman (Prov. 5) enrapture you?"

WISE PEOPLE FEAR AND BUILD:

Proverbs reminds us, **He who walks (as a companion) with wise men is wise, but he wo associates with (self-confident) fools is (a fool himself and) shall smart for it** (AMP). you are responsible to add wise people to your relationships.

Stay away from this wayward and foolish people and thinking, or you will lose your dignity and self-respect and will give your years over to the power of strangers and foreigners. Prov 5:7-14, **Now then, my sons** (that's you and me, literally 'the builder of the family name'), **listen to me; do not turn aside from what I say (pay attention and do it)**. Only Godly wisdom will enable him to exercise a correct thinking ability to resist the effects of this immoral (foolish) woman.

Keep to a path far from her, do not go near the door of her house, lest you give your best strength to others and your years to one who is cruel, lest strangers feast on your wealth and your toil enrich another man's house. Having forfeited his self-respect and exhausted his resources the foolish person then groans the long litany of "if only." If only I hadn't gone my own way, if only I had listened. But this realization usually comes too late — his reputation is ruined; his health is gone. **You will say, "How I hated discipline! How my heart spurned correction! I would not obey my teachers or listen to my instructors. I have come to the brink of utter ruin in the midst of the whole assembly"** (Prov. 5 NIV).

Wisdom = the ability to put Scriptural knowledge and understanding to use, and discernment to distinguish right from wrong and to choose the correct road.

As the earliest Christians continued in the apostles' doctrine and fellowship, FEAR came upon them... the result? Many wonders and signs were done by the Apostles!!! (Acts. 2:42,43). The bedrock consequence of established Apostolic doctrine is FEAR (reverential terror of the sacred).

In order to avoid being foolishly ensnared, we must guard our thinking. We need to correctly direct our thought processes into accurate discernment and think harmoniously

THE 1ST STEP—
Fear

with Godly wisdom. Believers don't need to hear another message – they need to seek this new model and be empowered for LIFE. Wisdom is that model. God sent us a job — that of building our temple. Matthew 7:24-27 tells us that the wise man builds his house upon a rock. He builds with legitimate and correct philosophies, values, and motives. He builds with decrees that unleash Divine laws upon the earth. He operates out of a system of Godly understanding. He resonates What and Who God is. Then no matter what calamity comes his way, his house can't fall down.

The "man of sin" (the Adamic memory) sits proudly in our temple claiming to be "in charge." The truth is that in times past our soul gravitated toward foolishness and adapted to whatever we put inside. Now, we have to reverse the process -- to reckon that old man dead. Once and for all, realize that the fallen nature cannot inherit the kingdom. It can't be fixed. Build a foundational resolve that refuses to be hampered by returning to emotional soulish battles. We see repeated throughout scripture — and once again in Proverbs 14:1 — that every wise woman buildeth her house. It is a TOTALLY NEW place. She is ALIVE unto Christ! She demonstrates *godliness*.

THE HOUSE ITSELF:

What's it about living in a nice house? Haggai spent a lot of time working on his own personal dwelling. The Lord told him (Hag. 1:9), "My house is in ruins." The building of the temple and the rebuilding of the temple typify the inner building of God's dwelling — He wants to live in us. He wants our attention to be given to the condition of His dwelling. Godly wisdom teaches us to dismantle our long-entrenched and contentious mind-sets so that no false principality can be activated within. We need to carefully plan the kinds of wood that we choose, the colors we paint, and the embroidered curtains that we use to decorate the vessels of honor within our soul.

Scores of Scriptures use the metaphor of the house. The evil woman's *house* leads down to hell (Prov. 2:18). Set your *house* in order (Is. 28). Storms will beat on your *house* (Matt. 7:25). Remember, a *house* divided cannot stand (Matt. 12:25). Even a bishop must continue to rule (manage) his own *house* (1 Tim. 3:4). Haggai tells that when the God's *house* was completed the unexpected happened – God's glory fell (Hag. 2:7).

For years, we've been at the quarry having our hardened hearts fashioned into lively stones. Before long, we must be fitted together with neither the sound of hammers nor tools. The process of building our lives with quality construction is supernatural. **And the house, while it was being built, was built of stone prepared at the quarry, and there was neither hammer nor axe nor any iron tool heard in the house while it was being built** (1 Kings 6:7).

The Happiness of Finding Wisdom

THE 1ST STEP—
Fear

THE TWO MINDS, THE TWO WIVES:

And, once again we realize that there are two women in the book of Proverbs: the wise wife and foolish wife (also called the strange woman). As believers we respond with either of these two kinds of mind – <u>as one type of wife or the other</u>. The spotless Bride or the foolish — one who lives in bondage or freedom; life or death; being contentious or prepared. Notice how Proverbs to compares these two types of believers:

<u>FOOLISH (UNRENEWED MIND)</u> <u>RELIGIOUS & LIMITED THINKING</u>	<u>WISE (RENEWED MIND)</u> <u>BELIEVER EXPERIENCING LIFE</u>
The Spirit of whoredom. Harlot	Bride, ideal wife
Bond	Free
Carnal	Mind of Christ
Price of a loaf of bread (6:26)	Price far above rubies (31:10)
She is rottenness to the bones (12:4)	She is health to all (4:13, 22)
She is lazy (9)	She works diligently (31:13)
Her end is wormwood (5:4)	She is a tree of life (3:18)
She tears down her house (7:27, 14:1)	She builds (9, 14:1)
She calls to the simple (7:7)	She calls to sons of men (8:4)
She acts in the twilight (7:9)	She moves in the day (4:18)
She wears harlots clothes (7:11)	She wears linen and purple (31:22)
She steals and robs (6:26, 7:110)	She has her own bread & wine (9)
She roams and is wayward (4:16, 7:11-12)	(She gets up early and works (31:15)
She sits at the door (9)	She stands at the top of high places
She calls from the street corner in the dark	She calls from the open place
She offers mixed wine (23:30)	She offers mingled wine (9:2)
She says "turn aside" (9:17)	She says, "follow the steps of Godly men (2:20)
Her house is empty (7:19)	Her house is furnished (9, 31:13)
Her husband left (7:19-20)	Her husband sits at the gate (31:11)'
Her mouth is a deep ditch (23:27)	Her mouth is wisdom (8:6)
She seduces & entices (5:3, 2:16, & 6:24)	She speaks truth (8:6, 31:26)

The Happiness of Finding Wisdom

THE 1ST STEP—
Fear

Her path leads astray (7:25)	Her path leads to favor (18:22)
Her lips drip honey	She mingles honey with spices
FOOLISH	**WISE**
Grieves his mother (10:1)	Makes his father glad
Profits nothing (2)	Delivers others from death
They cast away their desire (3)	Never famished, desire fulfilled
His hands make poor (4)	His hands make rich
Violence covers his mouth (6)	Blessings are on his head
His name will rot (7)	His memory is blessed
His way is perverted (9)	He walks securely
Violence in his words	His mouth is a well of life
A rod for his back (13)	Wisdom is on his mouth
He nears destruction (14)	He lays up knowledge
His wages lead to sin 16	His labor leads to life
He goes astray (17)	He is in the way of life
He talks a lot (19)	He restrains his lips
Sports to do mischief (23)	He lives in wisdom
Proclaims foolishness (23)	Conceals (hides) knowledge

**Your next assignment: make your own list like that above for chapters 11, 12, and 13.

The Happiness of Finding Wisdom

THE 2ND STEP—

LEARNING HOW TO "GET KNOWLEDGE"

We just learned that in order to get wisdom we must first fear the Lord. Now, we realize that not only is the fear of the Lord the <u>beginning</u>. Proverbs also says, **"The fear of the Lord is the <u>beginning</u> of <u>knowledge</u>"** (1:7). In comparison we read Prov 9:13, **a foolish woman is clamorous; she is simple, and <u>knows nothing</u>** (she has a lot of facts but hasn't collected any Truth; she's ever restless).

Wisdom = <u>knowing</u> the infinite measure of the greatness of God Himself indwelling our lives.

Knowledge is the <u>second step</u> to Wisdom's house. Accurate knowledge accumulates Godly and pertinent facts about a topic or situation. **Prov. 2:5 Then shalt thou understand the <u>fear</u> of the Lord** (that's first — and then the consequence) **and find the <u>knowledge</u> of God** (KJV). Reverential fear leads to finding knowledge. That fear manifests itself in an obedient and disciplined life that confesses and forsakes sin (28:18), and does right (21:3). Godly fear leads to true knowledge that only comes by revelation (3:6).[1]

GOD'S FOUR TYPES OF KNOWLEDGE:

1. THE KNOWLEDGE OF CHRIST.

Eph. 1:17, **That the God of our Lord Jesus Christ... may give unto you the spirit of wisdom and revelation in the <u>knowledge of him</u>** (KJV). The word knowledge is "epiginosko" (#1921, 1922) which means being mature, probing and deep, complete, accurate, thorough, and precise. We must obtain a knowledge of Christ that displays these qualties. (See also 1 Cor. 1:5.)

2. THE KNOWLEDGE OF GOD'S WILL.

Col. 1:9 ...(We) do not cease to pray for you, and to desire that ye might be filled with the <u>knowledge of his will</u> in all wisdom and spiritual understanding; that ye might walk worthy of the Lord unto all pleasing, being fruitful in every good work, and increasing in the <u>knowledge of God</u> (KJV). Paul prays that we might know God's will in all "spiritual wisdom" and then do His will "with all spiritual understating."

---

1. Ibid, Zuck, pg. 43.

THE 2ND STEP—
Learning how to "GET knowledge"

3. THE KNOWLEDGE OF TRUTH.
1 Tim. 2;4, **Who will have all men to be saved, and to come unto the knowledge of the truth** (KJV). His word is truth and it makes us free (Jn. 8:32).

4. THE KNOWLEDGE OF EVERY GOOD THING WE HAVE IN CHRIST.
Philemon 1:6, **That the communication of thy faith may become effectual by the acknowledging of every good thing which is in you in Christ Jesus** (KJV). Each of us must know and acknowledge the calling that Christ has placed within us (see also 2 Tim. 4:5, Col. 4:17).

KNOWING God isn't just knowing *about* Him, or having had an encounter with Him years ago. Knowing means to intimately and completely trust His Word so much that you incorporate that lifestyle into your character. Knowing God incorporates knowing who you are in Him. It means that you walk in the fullness of that revelation. It means to walk away from the foolishness of the immoral woman — to not be like her. TO BE WISE.

KNOWLEDGE
FEAR OF THE LORD

True knowledge issues out of awesome reverence of the Lord. Knowledge continues the process of bringing that *eusibea* (reverent fear of the Lord or *godliness*) into action in our everyday lives. Therefore, the next thing we have to do is gather KNOWLEDGE.

KNOWING GOD WAS LOST:
Before the fall, the first couple walked and talked with God… they KNEW Him. Everything they could ever need was on the Tree of LIFE — Wisdom hung there on that tree. Their soul-realm (mind, will, and emotions) functioned healthily. This first couple knew right from wrong, otherwise they couldn't be held accountable for not doing it. But, they wanted more.

Gen 3:6 When the woman saw that the fruit of the tree (of the Knowledge of Good and Evil) **was good for food and pleasing to the eye, and also desirable for gaining WISDOM, she took some and ate it.** NIV The temptation concerned what they put inside themselves. (They were both there -- and both made wrong decisions.)

       1. The food they wanted to eat.
       2. The things they wanted to observe.
       3. The information they wanted to know.

The Happiness of Finding Wisdom

THE 2ND STEP—
Learning how to "GET knowledge"

The first man and woman lived the supernatural life because of being created in the image of The Life-giving Spirit (1 Cor. 15:45). They could eat from all the other wonderful trees in the garden. But Adam and the woman chose the serpent's favorite — they longed for the tree of human wisdom and <u>lost the wisdom of God</u>. They didn't understand the impending havoc and confusion that would result from walking in the flesh and being ruled by worldly good and evil. If this first couple had eaten of the Tree of Life, they would have lived forever and would have maintained purpose-driven power over their flesh and over their mind.

The Lord God told them that if they ate of the tree of the KNOWLEDGE of Good and Evil, they would "surely die." That literally says, "in dying you shall surely die. The fall had three deaths – that of the spirit, soul, and body. When their minds knew good and evil, their bodies began to age, and they spiritually lost communion with God. They lost their perspective of eternal purpose. They hid and were afraid.

The ability of choice was present. Yet they chose wrongly. They partook of the forbidden tree — that Tree of the KNOWLEDGE of Good and Evil. Soon, the desire for food, sensory satisfaction, and worldly wisdom took ascendancy over the fear (awesome reverence) of God's spoken Word. And, they ate. They chose to listen to the voice of carnality rather than take dominion. Their consequences came to all of us — and even this very day we choose whether we will also eat of the worldly systems or not.

A veil came upon humanity's mind – a thick separation — like a cataract or dense opaque clouding that divided between the soul and spirit.[1] The once harmonious soul and the spirit now disassociated into two worlds that came into tension, the God-like nature and the mind of man. Disobedience disconnected humanity from a relationship with God. Where they had once walked and talked with their Creator in the cool of the day, now they ate what they wanted and called it education. Humanism became the knowledge of man. Human thinking seemed right… And, in the day that we eat of the Tree of Knowledge, we shall surely die… (Gen. 2:17).

The original plan was for believes to rule, reign, and have dominion – that was God's intention for creation from the beginning. Adam and the woman should have tended their garden. The fall brought the loss of LIFE. If we continue to eat of the wrong tree and exist in a fallen state of carnality, we give ground and reality to the devil. If we're on guard about the things we digest (eat), the things we see, and the things we learn -- then each temptation becomes an opportunity to learn and overcome.

---

1. 2 Cor. 3:14 For those who turn to the Lord, the veil is removed.

The Happiness of Finding Wisdom

THE 2ND STEP—
Learning how to "GET knowledge"

THE DEVIL:
If we persist in stroking our OLD NATURE, we nullify the work of the cross and once again, the devil has power. But, he only has power IF we allow it. Remember that Jesus totally destroyed the works of the devil. For those who WALK IN THE SPIRIT — the cross did it! It is FINISHED for those who accept full redemption for themselves.

(Lots of super spiritual people don't want to hear about this part. They really want to hang onto their religious methods of extended battling, crying, and pleading.) But, here's the essence of the Gospel... after Jesus died, He went to hell and "triumphed over it." He took the keys of death and hell. If I really believe that "HE who is in me is greater" — then I don't have to waste my time with lengthy "religious" preoccupation.

We see the serpent in the garden become a dragon in Revelation – because fearful and superstitious believer have empowered him to grow in their minds. Isaiah maintains that when we see the devil, we'll say, "this is it? He's just a shriveled up little thing... defeated." We must wonder why we make him so big... Remember the snake that crawled out of the fire and onto Paul's hand? He just shook it off — with no rebuke and no intercession!

> * Two thieves died along side Jesus. One represented the Adamic fallen nature – he said, "Remember me." Jesus responded, "Today, you will be with me in Paradise." That thief represents the fallen nature that was erased by the cross. But there was a second thief who taunted and questioned Jesus' with the very same words as the devil did– (see Luke 4:9, 23:39). This thief (who represents the devil) DIED at Golgotha. The thief in John 10:10 is not the thief anymore – he's destroyed.

Either Jesus came to destroy the devil — or the work of the cross has failed. For this avowed intention (purpose) was <u>the Son of God</u> manifest, that he might destroy (sever, dismantle forever) the works of the evil one (1 Jn. 3:8 AMP). His PURPOSE was to utterly annihilate the system of darkness. That's it. He did it. Surely He has purposed it and so it shall stand (see Isaiah 14:24-27). To Christians, he's disarmed. He can only make suggestions...like, "Hath God said?" He talks a lot, but he has blank bullets.

NEGATIVE THOUGHTS IN THE CARNAL MIND:
- <u>Negative thinking</u>, low self worth. "I'll never do it."
- <u>Apprehension of others</u>. "They won't let me do it." If your motivation is built upon what others think, then you allow them to have power over your life. Realize that no one should control you.

The Happiness of Finding Wisdom

THE 2ND STEP—
Learning how to "GET knowledge"

- Sickness <u>and weakness</u>. "I can't do it; I'm too tired."
- <u>Anxiety and fear.</u> "I'm afraid of them." *Negative fear* = to consider or expect with alarm an unpleasant or strong emotion caused by the anticipation or awareness of danger. Every event of fear dissipates the momentum of your progress.
- <u>Victim mentality.</u> "I'm the only one." The feelings of always being vulnerable twists your perspective and grips you with weakness.
- <u>Limitations and ordinariness</u>. "I'm not good enough." Listen, no one is. But, God is good enough for all of us.
- <u>Poverty and tribulation</u>. "I'll never be able to do it."
- <u>Aimless reality</u>. "What's the point?"
- <u>Dislike of people</u>. "Everybody hates me."
- <u>Wasted life.</u> "What's the use?" No excitement. Senses dulled.
- <u>Controlling thoughts</u>. "I can't help it."
- <u>Doubt and unbelief</u>, "I wonder why?"

John tells us a pointed example of the power of suggestion on the unrenewed mind. (Jn. 13:2), **"So during supper, Satan having <u>already put the thought</u> of betraying Jesus in the heart of Judas Iscariot..."** (Amplified Bible). Notice the sudden infiltration of unresisted thought into the heart of Judas? Thoughts can come to us like that, anytime, any day. But those random thoughts can't penetrate a renewed and activated mind.

Also, notice that Satan is not all powerful. He's the prince of this world (Eph. 2:2) -- but you're no longer of this world (Jn. 17;14)! Satan didn't know who Jesus was when He was born, nor where He was born. That's why all the baby boys were killed in Bethlehem. Satan is not all-powerful. He would not have crucified Jesus if he had known the divine plan (1 Cor. 2:8, Col. 1:26). Satan cannot read your mind and he does not know your thoughts. The wicked on can not touch us (1 Jn. 5:18).

Now is come salvation, and strength, and the kingdom of our God, and the power of Christ; FOR OUR ACCUSER (SATAN) IS CAST DOWN... and we overcome him by the blood of the lamb, and by the word of our testimony (Rev. 12:10-11). If we do not believe that the devil is cast down, then we have problems.

The Happiness of Finding Wisdom

THE 2ND STEP—
Learning how to "GET knowledge"

DEFEAT ONLY COMES FROM ACTIVATED MEMORIES OF THE CARNAL MIND.

- Carnality allows the power of the "law of sin" to reign over the human will.
- Carnal thinking causes our BODY to be sick or tired.
- Carnal thinking causes our SOUL to be depressed, angry, jealous, and exhausted. Then, we feel excessive worry and fear about the things we don't want to happen.
- Carnal thinking causes our SPIRIT to become lawless (Matt. 24:12). This lawlessness rises up against the God in us that rules our temple.
- Carnal thinkers don't know God's ways.

Have you ever wondered if your mind operates in this world's systems? Ask yourself:

- "Is my mind…" Blank? (An empty or blank mind waits for someone else or something else to activate it.)
- Inactive or lazy? (This type wants to do something, but never does.)
- Scattered or inattentive? (This causes you to lose confidence and have no self-worth.)
- Indecisive or unrestrained? (This means you rarely finish what you start.)
- Can I make a decision and stick with it? Do I waiver with double mindedness (James 1:8)?
- Do I believe the Bible one day and not the next?
- Do I sometimes desire to run with the world? Carnal mindedness is death (Rom. 8:6).
- Is my mind unbridled? Do I gossip, slander, jest, and never listen? (See Ps. 141:3).
- Do I crave external aids? Do I repeatedly want medication, sleeping pills, liquor, or drugs? (See Prov. 3:24, Ps. 127:2).

If you answered "yes: to any of the above questions, then you probably are dealing with a carnal mind – and the law of sin and death is probably not fully reckoned with.

You will <u>not</u> understand the spiritual realm with a carnal mind.

The Happiness of Finding Wisdom

THE 2ND STEP—
Mastery over carnal activities:

**Write Romans 8:7, Isaiah 55:7-8, and list what caused you to have "carnal feelings."

As you target these negative emotions, you can ask the following questions:
>When was the first time that I felt these feelings?
>Who and/or what triggers these feelings?
>Should I feel differently?
>Should I continue to feel this way, what could happen?
>Am I willing to release this feeling and let go of the issues that created this negativity?
>What could happen if I don't let go?
>What should I do right now?
>Is it really the devil? Or is it me?

Carnality is incompatible with the NEW CREATION IN CHRIST. Become aware of your rights as a believer; become secure and stand without wavering. Wisdom from above is easily entreated. The Spirit world accurately interacts with humankind in specific ways. The spirit of God enters into the physical world through the spirit of a believer and is interpreted by his/her wholesome mind.

It's time to recognize the regenerating power of the new birth -- to embrace the TOTAL Life of Jesus Christ as our Lord and Savior. It denigrates the miracle of salvation when believers constantly struggle and miss the target of maturity (1 Cor. 14:20 NKJ).

Carnality = the hostile battle that opposes the will of God.

MASTERY OVER CARNAL ACTIVITIES:

People generally base their actions on the way they believe things to be instead of identifying with the triumph of Jesus over Satan (1 Jn. 4:4, Col. 2:15, 1 Co. 15:57, 2 Co. 2:14)). We cannot "cast out" fear or discouragement. We must "overcome" negative emotions by thinking redemptive thoughts (Rom. 12:21). There's no need to intercede for God to keep His promises. JUST BELIEVE THEM!

- We must expose the lie that caused us to believe incorrectly. What was it that caused us to discredit the victory of the Cross? Doubt and disbelief, like arrows shot into the air, can disappear or land anywhere they want. We

The Happiness of Finding Wisdom

THE 2ND STEP—
Mastery over carnal activities:

      must be alert to our own negativity and minimize the impact of these thought patterns coming back to life again.

- We must learn from our mistakes and move on. The better choice is to go toward resolution -- resolve to embrace the redemptive facts of the Word, instead of doubting. Remember that we're free only to change our present and future. Life has only one direction, and that's straight ahead.

- There's no reason to fear the devil -- Christ LIVES in your house (Jn. 14:23)! Resist the devil (with the facts of the Word of God), and HE WILL flee from you (Jam. 4:7).

Satan's only power against believers is the power that they concede to him. He has no power of his own.

THE INTELLECT (KNOWING) THAT NEEDS TO BE REDEEMED:

Most would define knowledge as being "smart" or "intellectual." Of course, we all know that there's nothing more counterproductive than conceitedness of our own knowing (1 Cor. 8:1-3). Those who are wise in their own eyes have an exaggerated opinion of their own sufficiency. We can actually perish for the lack of the *right kind of knowledge* (Hos. 4:6).

Even as the angry crowds crucified Him, Jesus said, "Forgive them Father, for they <u>KNOW NOT</u> what they do..." Even today, our habitual patterns of carnal thinking causes us to NOT KNOW. We question what God says in our lives. We're lured into that wrong tree of human reasoning and knowledge of the mind. While there's nothing intrinsically wrong with mental ability or academic learning, we often crave for undesirable knowledge. We all must radically turn away from distractions and choose to eat of the right tree and have LIFE. Let's look at a list of intellectual capacities that we must develop into a renewed mind of "right," redemptive (wise) thought.

- The intellects can repeat back something, i.e., rote learning. To memorize. Memory = the willful effort to remember facts and information (Jn. 14:26). Recalling opinions, beliefs, and conclusions.

The Happiness of Finding Wisdom

THE 2ND STEP—
Mastery over carnal activities:

- The intellect gathers data from reading, empirical research, and conversations, etc.
- The intellect creates data by using induction and deduction to generate new data.
- The intellect fills in some gaps in our "knowing." It assembles and categorizes similar facts.
- The intellect helps us decide which decision is most likely to be productive.
- The intellect provides information for response.
- The intellect verifies data. For example, if we receive a message that tells us that the sun will not rise tomorrow, our logic rightly disagrees.
- The intellect formats data for logical analysis.
- The intellect dimensionalizes our understanding of data. In other words, the intellect it is like a computer which can present the word, "cat," on its monitor. Eventhough it may not know what a cat is, the mind can translate that word into the mental dimension.
- The intellect examines our emotional experiences, to view them from its own mental perspective — a perspective that adds a valuable dimension to our understanding.

Because our intellect holds accumulated information, we can tap it to make future decisions on other matters. We store information and facts in the subconscious memory, then we can bring that information into our consciousness for use. Depending on that particular memory, we can benefit or be hindered.

So here we have this premise again: The memory stores accumulated knowledge – but only as we perceive it – whether true or not. The memory retains both true and false information, both positive and negative experiences. The memory cannot discern truth from falsehood. It just remembers. Only the spiritually conscious mind can begin to filter and discern truth and falsehood – <u>and only if it is assigned the task</u>. If we don't control what goes into the memory, then it's possible for unrestrained thoughts to manipulate us into false assumptions and conclusions. If we continue to hold onto unchecked information, it gives ground to our carnality (weakness). Only when we realize we are in bondage to negative memories, can we allow God to renew them.

A person can be extremely intelligent — and still not be wise.

The Happiness of Finding Wisdom

THE 2ND STEP—
Mastery over carnal activities:

> To maintain discerning perspective, Paul said that the love of Christ surpassed all knowledge (Eph. 3:19). True knowledge always presents itself through love.

Wise believers discern/distinguish between the general gathering of information and the kind of knowledge required for productive LIFE. They have learned to position themselves into a place of learning beyond books. If we define knowledge as a means to achieve something of a material value, then we do not understand the full concept of this word. We must move past the function of the basic intellect into a renewed mind with wise reasoning. We DECIDE to learn new productive, Scriptural truth -- and unlearn wrong information. Before we move on from this point, we should appreciate the ability to relearn, to function intelligently, and to retain information for further development.

> *"The Scriptures do not make the mistake of confusing wisdom with other mental capacities, or giving wisdom less than its central place."*
> -- Lawrence O. Richards

KNOWING ESTABLISHES A "RENEWED MIND"

There's a mighty fortress that stands through any storm --and that's a total change of character – a transformed mind. Transformed into the re-establishment of LIFE, the application of the perfect blood (life of His flesh) reforms our SOUL (1 Cor. 2:16, Eph. 4:23, Phil. 2:5, 2 Tim. 1:7).

**Write out Romans 12:1-3 and meditate about it in new creative ways:

The grace obtained from your initial salvation now allows you to comprehend and apprehend wisdom. Wisdom happens by building new thought patterns. That's what the Paul meant when he said that we are the circumcision made without hands, by "putting off" the sins of the flesh (Col, 2:11)… only YOU can "put it off." And only by revelation, can YOU "put on" that new man — not God, not your pastor, not prayer, not your parents, not even the mailman can do it for you. No you do it. How many times has your coat jumped out of the coat closet and thrown itself onto your body? No, you "put on" the new man.

> *This renewed mind is not an option; it's a command.*

We can't add the new man on top of the old man. NO. Old thoughts must die. Our success and happiness depend on the quality of our new thoughts prevailing (Prov. 23:7). Success begins on the inside and later manifests itself on the outside. Every action is first conceived in our mind. New thoughts precede new actions. Knowing precedes understanding.

The Happiness of Finding Wisdom

THE 2ND STEP—
Mastery over carnal activities:

Jesus intends to exchange His SOUL realm attributes with us – to give us His mind – the way He thinks about things, the way He feels about things, the way He reacts, the way He makes decisions. That's what LIFE is all about. **Let this mind** (attitude) **be in you** (Phil. 2:5) -- it's a command, not a request!

PRESENT

Now, let's review what you wrote earlier (Romans 12:1-3). **Present your <u>body</u> as a living sacrifice.**

Willingly and willfully become moved to do acts of the heart and tasks of obedience out of the energy of love. Your body becomes a spirit enactment of service.

Don't be Conformed to this world.

NOT CONFORMED

Conformed = "to continually apply pressure until it takes the shape of the mold desired by the one applying pressure." Don't be <u>conformed</u> to this world. 1 John 2:5-16 tells us to love not the world, or as the Amplified version says not to have, "craving for sensual gratification and greedy longings of the mind that consume one with desire." Don't act like unredeemed.

Be transformed to God's way of thinking.

TRANSFORMED

- Totally changed into a new entity and identity.
- Be different than before. Change the inside.
- Allow the fruit to grow with integrity.
- Become reprogrammed by God's purposes.
- Create a lifestyle behavior that depicts spiritual reality.
- Break the former principles that ruled the thought life.
- Reconstruct the order of logic and the concept of Truth.

Be renewed in your <u>mind</u>.

RENEWED

- Restore to the original state of freshness, or beauty.

The Happiness of Finding Wisdom

THE 2ND STEP—
Mastery over carnal activities:

- Control the responses to incorrect emotions and feelings.
- Posses new responses that spiritually act with accuracy and precise principles.
- React with conscious willingness and readiness.
- Respond with enlivened movement, sense of direction, and finalized destination.
- Possess accuracy in Spiritual arenas. Have fresh revelation. Articulate and express activated and exact giftings.

Find the will of God. (It can be found).

FINDING

- Notice how the scriptures tie together the ideas of renewing the mind with knowing God's will.
- Be purpose driven.
- Desire to live sacrificially to accomplish the will of God.
- Live in harmony with beliefs and actions.
- Live as much as possible, without intentional sin.
- Manifest in behavior the image and standard of God. Be a witness with your life.
- Complete your purpose.

The gift of our yielded lives is the acceptable worship to God.

What does Romans say is acceptable to God? We come to him on his terms. Look up Romans 12:1-4 in NIV translation and explain spiritual worship: Write Matt. 4:1, & Rom. 6:13. Discuss how well you control your emotions and your tongue. Is it easy or is it hard? Are your feelings easily hurt? What kind of friends do you hang around? How can a renewed mind help you to know God's will? How can a renewed mind help you "build your spiritual house" and achieve your destiny? How can a renewed mind help you to understand God's word, and to apply it? How can a renewed mind help you to know the depths of God's love? (1 Cor. 2:10-11)?

THE 2ND STEP—
Mastery over carnal activities:

Right knowing comes from a transformed mind. That means we stop blaming the devil and take responsibility for our situations. We can trust God. Trust means to approach the conditions in our life with a sense of hope, faith, and belief that there is a reason for all that is happening. Jeremiah reminds us (29:11), **For I know the thoughts that I think toward you, says the LORD, thoughts of peace and not of evil, to give you a future and a hope.** When we KNOW that God has good thoughts concerning us, then trust happens beyond our five senses, beyond the physical awareness. God is in charge. The following are some rewards for having a healed mind:

BELIEF IS A SOUL REALM FUNCTION:

The awareness and articulation of spirituality is an activity of the SOUL. God told Ezekiel, **"Look with your eyes and hear with your ears and fix your heart** (mind) **on everything I show you..."** (40:4). Then Ezekiel declared this soul realm comprehension to the people. That's the activity of the redeemed intellect. The ability to accurately interpret input. What did Ezekiel see, hear about, and fix his mind upon??? Why yes... it's **THE TEMPLE**!!!

You the believer must fix your eyes, your ears, and your heart on your temple. You must tend and guard your own garden (Eden, the paradise of God where He walks and talks; your temple where God abides).

KNOWING MEANS WE CAN IMAGINE CORRECTLY:

Because of past misapplication, Christians have become hesitant to use their imaginations. However, the act of really KNOWING God demands that we take time to dream and imagine (Joel 2:28). Dreams are what the future is made of. That's why we take time to imagine what should be, could be, or 'otta be. Imagination means to willfully picture (mentally imagine) the facts we know and the thoughts we think. This activity should put us in participation with those thoughts. Renewed imagination can work to our benefit.

> Develop God-given imagination for the good. For example, we can learn to imagine the meaning of the songs we sing. The more we practice — the easier it becomes. Try to picture the Bible stories and view yourself inside the situations. Feel the excitement of being personally involved. Perhaps you can hear the conversations of the characters. Enhance your mental picture by asking questions. Expand the Bible to solve present day situations.

> Visualize the success of making a right choice. For example, picture yourself as an organized person, or see yourself with a great job. What is your picture?

The Happiness of Finding Wisdom

THE 2ND STEP—
Mastery over carnal activities:

> Realize (know and understand) the potential of God's promises. The more you imagine positively, the more your mind gets stronger. The stronger you build your house, the quicker you can break bad habits.

KNOWING MEANS THAT WE CAN CREATE NEW HABITS:

God gave us all the particular (and often peculiar) capacity to have habits. Usually, we don't even realize that we have habits. But, we all do… There was a time when it wasn't easy to drive a car, but we learned how to shift gears by practice, and now we can do it while talking, listening to the radio, and eating – no problem. Once we've acquired a new habit, then our highly complex behavior patterns unconsciously start taking over.

Hebrews 5:13 tells us that these Christians had heard a lot of teaching but they had not benefited because they didn't consistently use what they already KNEW. **"But solid food** (mashed potatoes and steak) **is for the mature who because of practice** (habitually doing it over and over) **have their senses trained to discern between good and evil."** See that? We become mature by training our senses over and over again to habitually respond to what we know is true. The practice of discerning good and evil is vital.

Our current use of habituated responses cannot be underestimated. That's how God created humanity to live. We must stop to examine our habit patterns and then evaluate them. There's only one way to change. We have to recognize the need for change and patiently retrain ourselves by repetition — that's line upon line, precept by precept, here a little, there a little. Pattern by pattern.

> **Tell the meaning of Mark 9:23 in your own words: Can a leopard change his spots? No. Can you change? Absolutely. It's never too late. You can live more efficiently. Stop cussing. Get up earlier. Lose weight. Stop being depressed. Pray. Yes. Most researchers say that it takes about three weeks of daily work to create a new habit. Then, it takes about three more weeks to be really comfortable in it. So where will you start?**

"RIGHT KNOWING" ACTIVATES THE "LAW OF LIFE:"

Paul talks a lot about the "law of sin" that hounded him. He wished he could do good, but the power to do good wasn't there. Sometimes, even Paul may have wanted to yield to sin without resisting -- flesh drew his soul towards sin and death. For a time, he could not escape this inner frustration. But, Paul had revelation. He assured us of a different law working — the much <u>greater</u> law of the Spirit of LIFE. **Write this law (ROM. 8:1-3):

The Happiness of Finding Wisdom

THE 2ND STEP—
Mastery over carnal activities:

- Our responses ultimately lead to who we become. God intends that our mind be yielded and responsive to His Spirit.
- We must choose the law of sin and death or the Law of the Spirit of Life.
- We can deliberately change our thoughts and choose to meditate on suitable subjects concerning LIFE.
- We can willfully focus our thoughts on God's Word. (Rom. 8:5).
- We can concentrate on what needs to be done at this moment.
- We can reflect the image and likeness of Christ.

**Write 1 Thess. 5:21, Col. 1:9-10, 3:2, and Phil. 2:11-13.

Wrong thinking produces a lack of discernment, and then our confused mind refuses to cooperate with God. Because our thinking affects our emotions and our decisions, we must choose our thoughts carefully. <u>The Spirit of Life</u> brings release. I am dead unto sin and ALIVE! Paul victoriously declares his freedom because the Law of the Spirit of Life has already been acquired and completed. Now, he tells us what to do — not just what NOT to do....he says to WALK IN LIFE.

RIGHT KNOWING PUTS THE SPIRIT OF LIFE INTO OUR MINDS.

Once we KNOW about the Spirit of LIFE, it begins to deliver us into present truth (2 Pet. 1:12), which focuses on Jesus and the NEW CREATION. We become released from sin-conscious messages. The early apostles called any legalistic exhortation "another Gospel" (Gal. 1:6). We aren't supposed to continuously worry about dying... we reckon (believe that it is accomplished) ourselves dead to sin and ALIVE unto Christ.

The Spirit of LIFE encourages us to look into the "glass" or "mirror" of the Word and see the NEW MAN. Why look! We have single eyed focus (Matt. 6:22-24). The face we see becomes (literally) our face of the beginnings, or the "GENESIS FACE" (Gen. 1:26-28) — the face of original creation rule & dominion. The Spirit of Life propels us to higher standards. It allows us to incarnate the promises given. We become the womb of God's expression, the tabernacle in which the covenants become birthed to actuality.

We must work out how our mind will respond to outside commands — it depends upon the programming set within. Agreement with God's precepts opens us to the Supreme overruling power of LIFE. When our mind and heart agree, then we also find Godly influence upon other areas of our thought life: Proper knowing means we can optimize several abilities:

The Happiness of Finding Wisdom

THE 2ND STEP—
Mastery over carnal activities:

Meditation: = the repeating or muttering of a concept. It an also mean to chew like a cud, to remember over and over, to murmur, and to sigh. Joshua was instructed to meditate on the Book of the Law and to obey it (Josh 1:8). Psalms 1:2 says the "blessed man" meditates on God's law day and night. The psalmist also prayed that the meditation of his heart would be acceptable in God's sight (Ps 19:14). Paul, in 1 Tim 4:15, urged Timothy to meditate, or to carefully follow his instructions. (See also Phil 4:8 and Col 3:2.)

** Write out Deut. 8:2, Num. 15:39, & Prov. 3:1 and meditate.

Godly intuition = a strong knowing or perception to our spirit from the Spirit of God. This perception sends a message to the conscious mind of our redeemed soul.

Godly communion = a strong drawing into a relationship with the Spirit of God. A hunger for intimacy, or a deeper and stronger craving.

Godly conscience = a strong voice of approval or disapproval of our actions, conduct, or motivation. The conscience enforces our values and convictions (1 Jn. 3:19-22).

Right knowing of the Spirit of Life also brings:
- Sincere relationships.
- Physical health and long life.
- Freedom from false thoughts.
- Happiness, peace, and self-control.
- Faith and not fear.
- Abundant life.
- Expanded direction and vision.

Only the renewed mind can discern accurately. Only transformation can replace negative feelings with self-actualizing thoughts.

The Happiness of Finding Wisdom

THE 2ND STEP—
Mastery over carnal activities:

THE PAST:

You need to know three things about your past. Number one: You can't change the past. Number two: Some of the past is good -- some bad. Number three: All those experiences influence who you are today. Knowing these three things helps us to deal with the bad memories. Relate to the negative past as if it were long ago. Don't generate the enlarged or changed version of it. Unless you deal with the past, it could become a bitter root of expectancy – always reappearing in your tranquil garden. Here's what you have to do:

- Don't focus on past failures. Testify only with a triumphant report.

- Don't allow bitterness or comparisons to dwell.

- Ask God to forgive you for building a whole system around bad memories. Allow your new thought patterns to overcome your present ones. Force right words daily until they become a habit.

- Value the present moment, and don't give too much attention to the yesterdays. Go forward and face disappointments as one who has authority over it, not as one in bondage to that memory. It's a weed, something you don't want growing. Get rid of it. Don't just read this part. Do it.

- Forgive those involved who may have distorted your view of truth.

- Begin again to plan your life with vision and goals. Set your goals carefully and you will gain control. Center on the action necessary to accomplish new goals. With God's help you will no longer drift aimlessly. Be occupied with going forward. You'll soon become a good steward over the life for which you are accountable… "Well done."

- Set your mind on the "joy set before you" to finish the course.

A renewed mind discerns and analyzes the nature of the influencing thoughts. When the Holy Spirit divinely influences your renewed human spirit, then these messages process divinely inspired thoughts. You have the mind of Christ! Yes, you really do.

RIGHT KNOWING BRINGS ACCURACY:

Even the Pharisees had the right information, but their natural mind could not comprehend it, **"...You search the Scriptures diligently because you suppose and trust that you have eternal life through THEM.** (But those scholars missed the point. Jesus clarified it.) **And these very Scriptures testify about Me!"** (John 5:39).

The Happiness of Finding Wisdom

THE 2ND STEP—
Mastery over carnal activities:

Rational thought (The TREE OF KNOWLEDGE OF GOOD & EVIL) provided the Pharisees ample INFORMATION and KNOWLEDGE that was totally factual — but they missed the eternal Truth of knowing Jesus!

So, why do we study the Scriptures? Not just for information. We should study so that the Father might grant us **"a spirit of wisdom and REVELATION in the deep and intimate knowledge OF HIM..."**(Eph. 1:17). That's Christ revealing Himself... THAT revelation knowledge comes from a different Tree — the Tree of LIFE! [1]

THE KNOWLEDGE OF GOD:

Still, everywhere you look, the fallen nature produces uncertainty... people are depressed and unsure about what to do. Many are fearful of the unknown. These days it seems that almost everyone -- believer and nonbeliever -- falters with double mindedness. Isaiah describes those exceptions who walk without earthly fear. **And wisdom and knowledge shall be the stability of thy times....** (Isaiah 22:6a). Yes, only actuated wisdom and knowledge will stabilize your life. You can build your house upon this truth.

> *Oh, the depth of the riches of the wisdom and knowledge of God!*
> *How unsearchable his judgments, and his paths beyond tracing out!*
> (Rom. 11:33 NIV)

The Bible clearly states that God demanded people to have the knowledge of Him even more than He wanted sacrifices and burnt offerings (Hosea 6:6). Why is knowledge so important? Well, if we have it, then God can do great things through us. Habakkuk says that one day all the earth shall be filled with the knowledge of the glory of the Lord – even as the waters cover the sea (2:14). That means that the knowledge of God's glory will manifest everywhere and the world will know Him.

Hosea also says that we are destroyed by a lack of knowledge (4:6). He's talking about a lack of the kind of knowledge that transcends facts and becomes truth. A lack of meaningful knowledge is the reason why so many people are unhappy. Knowledge that is not pertinent causes us to make wrong decisions. Irrelevant knowledge produces an illusion that will not propagate. But, we are given grace to live according to God's will and this grace multiplies when we gain His knowledge. We can know ministry and not know God. Israel knew His works but not His ways (Ps. 103:7). Israel, God's chosen people, departed from the heritage of wisdom and followed false cultural principles. Likewise,

---

1. Concept from Fortune, D. ibid. March 14, 2000

THE 2ND STEP—
Mastery over carnal activities:

we can quote Scriptures and NOT *know* how to utilize them in our lives. We need God's knowledge.

When a wise man is instructed, he gets <u>knowledge</u>. (Prov 21:11)

<u>Knowledge</u> comes easily to the discerning. (Prov 14:6)

Jesus said, **If you continue** (abide, settle down into, make it part of your life) **in my Word, you shall <u>know the truth</u> and the truth shall make you free** (John 16:31-33). *Know* is the Greek word, *ginosko* meaning "progressive ever revealing knowledge." This knowing implies relationship between the one who knows and what is to be known. That kind of knowing brings liberty into our lives.

Wisdom longs to be discovered. She hides -- hoping to become planted deep inside our being. Psalms 51:6 says, **Behold, thou desirest truth in the inward parts: and in the hidden part thou shalt make me to <u>know</u> <u>wisdom</u>**. (KJV) God hides mysteries and it's the wisdom of kings to search it out (Prov. 25:2, 1 Cor. 2:7, Col. 2:3).

"Knowledge is horizontal. Wisdom is vertical -- it comes down from above."
　　　　　　Billy Graham

The profound experience of transitioning into this NEW CREATION reality connects us more actively to our Maker and one another. This quickened *knowing* enriches each present moment. Now, our lives have energized direction and structure, and our words have great impact. We go farther, we have a commanding presence, and we are a Biblical example of a Divine lifestyle. As NEW CREATION people, we define our own cosmos and *know* our right to rule in life. We attain new realities of the self-confidence of who we are in God. We provoke new levels of Truth and relate to others on a global level.

THE FURNITURE FOR YOUR HOUSE:

God cannot fully inhabit an immature house - even though seemingly successful spiritual activities may occur. Eph 1:23 declares that we (the church) are the *fullness* of Him who makes everything complete, and Who fills everything every where with Himself (AMP). That word "fullness" is *pleroma* which means "to finish and to furnish!" In other words, God -- the Grand Decorator -- furnishes us with Himself.

Yes, the Lord has it all planned, right down to the finest décor. Proverbs 24:4. **By <u>knowledge</u> the rooms are filled with all precious and pleasant riches**. What we have to do is gather that <u>knowledge</u> about what it takes to complete this project of building our lives according to His plan. What will we look like? Say it with me. "Jesus."

The Happiness of Finding Wisdom

THE 2ND STEP—
Mastery over carnal activities:

Knowledge becomes the second step of the temple that we must arise and build! **Wise men lay up <u>knowledge</u>...** Prov. 10:14a. Sometimes when we assimilate information that we have not known before, it will contradict other information already stored. We must choose to learn/ and learn to choose that which builds on Truth. Beloved, it matters what we know! That's why we must relearn incorrect thoughts and transform our mind. We insist upon remembering the good things of life -- not just the bad. We remember the good people and not just the ones who betrayed us. Truth accepted in our sub-conscious fills our rooms with precious and pleasant riches.

RETURNING TO RIGHT KNOWING:

Many modern churches present a living Jesus who comes to meet needs. Many unbelievers are still attracted to these particular churches because they nurture humanity issues. These churches are generally high-spirited, fun loving, and fast growing. They teach and preach ACTION and strategies. They teach us how to wrestle with the flesh (the OLD MAN), our problems, and the devil. They are need-oriented. Building centered.

However, the emerging apostolic church KNOWS the reality of the resurrected Lord and His full redemption. They seek LIFE. They're not just "doers" of the Word, but they BECOME the Word – they are a witness (to embody the principle, not just talk). Their hope is to BE an example, to BE prayer, to BE worship, to emulate Christ. These believers no longer come <u>through the veil.</u> The veil's been rent... They've come to where God alone dwells, where the cherubim faces touch. Here is the ONLY altar -- at The Mercy Seat of intense communion. No devil can exist in this Holy place. This NEW CREATURE, the image of the PATTERN SON, builds this temple with proclamations and decrees of the Word that forcefully advance the kingdom. This believer is "caught up" in His nature, consumed with Him, overshadowed by the Holy Spirit, and revealing Christ.

As we've said, true wisdom is not of man's words (1 Cor. 1:17). Jesus, the Wisdom of God (vs. 24), succeeded in living as the wisdom of God in this world. He, our forerunner, now gives that supernatural wisdom to us -- into our spirit, our soul, and our body. As (grown up) "sons of God," we choose to embrace the *purpose* of Jesus -- to maintain the destruction of every last vestige of the devil's influence in the church. We immediately destroy demonic structures and bring to pass that which has already been determined. There may be heard an occasional roar, but we eliminate his every effort.

In spite of that glorious truth, many still try to bring wholeness to that old nature which must ultimately be reckoned as dead... You see, the OLD MAN or the Adamic fallen nature is like Humpty Dumpty – it CAN NEVER be put back together again in the right way! It must DIE and then be transformed, regenerated, and made anew by the operative revelation into the image of the Son of God.

The Happiness of Finding Wisdom

THE 2ND STEP—.
Mastery over carnal activities:

There will always be Christians struggling to crucify their flesh, fighting the endless wars in their SOUL, unable to grasp the reality of the FINISHED work of the cross. We find that relentless soul realm struggle in people like Martha in verse 24 of John 11. Jesus told her the resurrection message and she just didn't comprehend it. She could only use her natural instincts to reply, "Yes, that will happen AFTER we die and go to heaven," not grasping the PRESENT reality of Jesus being the resurrection. It's happening now!

Jesus explained this concept very emphatically in Matt. 16:25, **"He who seeks to save HIS LIFE shall lose it..."** The word for save is 'sozo,' which means to protect, preserve, or make whole. Interestingly, the word life in this verse is *'psuche'* which, as you know by now, means the mind, or the SOUL! In other words, if we try to preserve our *fallen nature* (Adamic SOUL life), we'll lose it (destroy it fully and be left with nothing).

The God-life living through us KNOWS (intimately acquainted) God and the power (*dunamis* — capable of reproducing itself) of His resurrection (Phil. 3:1). Those believers have lost the fallen *psuche* (SOUL life). That's why Jesus said, **"...If any man will come after Me, let him deny himSELF** (old nature) **and take up his cross, and follow Me..."**(Matt. 16:24). This new focus changes from endlessly dying to self (that religious practice that leads to false humbleness and pride) – into becoming "conformable (in union) with his death." Now, we can follow His LIFE. That ultimate denial of our old man causes us to LIVE in the new – with a spiritually centered LIFE.[1]

Typologically, Eden (which means God's delight) is first and foremost a state of being. That's our goal -- to live in a place of God's delight, (Hepzibah- my delight is in her). The first humans lived in a garden with the incorruptible life of God available to them. They were masters over all things, living above sin, sickness, pain, or death. Eden revealed God's nature and purpose toward His creation – that humanity would rule and reign. God's desire was to "delight" Himself (for His pleasure we are created) in us.

The dynamic is that <u>Jesus waits</u> (ever interceding) in the heavenlies <u>for us to be delivered</u> from sin's desolation and to become the NEW CREATION living again in the Paradise garden of Eden, (Acts 17, Ezek. 36:35; and Jn. 1:12).[2] God (the Husbandman -- Jms 5:7) waits to forcefully reconnect and reap our fruit. We must "catch" the REVELATION of this true wisdom — that Christ LIVES His soul-LIFE fully through us, NOW in this lifetime. We become the Edenic landscaped garden where He comes to eat of our lives.

---

1. Initial ideas on Matt. 16:25 modified from Fortune, D. ibid. 2/19/- 3/25/00.
2. In the center of our ultimate Garden, God (see Song of Solomon) grows the Tree of Life – it is the Kingdom of Heaven GROWN within— (Mark 4:27).

The Happiness of Finding Wisdom

THE 2ND STEP—
Mastery over carnal activities:

THE 3RD STEP

UNDERSTANDING

This is a book about becoming happy because we find wisdom – wisdom is "the most important thing." But, there are three steps to get to wisdom. Prov 9:10 says, **The (#1) <u>fear</u> of the Lord is the beginning of wisdom: and the (#2) <u>knowledge</u> of the holy (One) is (#3) <u>understanding</u>**.

Once we have awesome reverence (fear, godliness) and accumulated accurate knowledge, we have a wonderful start. But it's not enough to just know about something. Now, we can build the next foundational layer in our Proverbs house of Wisdom– that of UNDERSTANDING.

Recently, I went to Egypt and learned a lot of facts. We traveled for days and I took notebooks full of notes. Trouble was – I didn't <u>understand</u> how to apply anything that I had learned! And so it is with most things that we KNOW… we still have to understand them. Until our KNOWING becomes transformed and activated, we'll not UNDERSTAND the things of God.

Many times we wait for the release of our future, but we must be willing to understand the places of our old nature that need to be removed – those broken boards and bricks that have built their own rigid walls. We need to understand how to incorporate what we know into a reality. We understand according to the purity of our heart motive. The voice of understanding calls us onward into deeper recesses of our temple, into the Holy of Holies.

Then opened He their <u>understanding</u>, that they might <u>understand</u> the scriptures,
Luke 24:45 (KJV)

UNDERSTANDING ESTABLISHES THE HOUSE:

Prov: 4:5, 7 demands … **<u>And with all thy getting get understanding</u>.** (God said to get it)… In other words, get the knowledge of God and then understand it. Paul instructed Timothy **Consider what I say, and may the Lord give you <u>understanding</u> in all things.**[1]

THE 3RD STEP
Understanding

The consequences of obtaining correct knowledge leads you to *"understand"* what you know – otherwise, what you know won't do you any good. It's better to learn a little bit and understand that part — than to get a college degree and not understand how to use any of it. It's not what you eat that does you good... but what you digest. Living in wisdom therefore becomes the exercise and practice of understanding. **Prov 24:3 Through wisdom is an house builded; and by <u>understanding</u> it is established** (KJV).

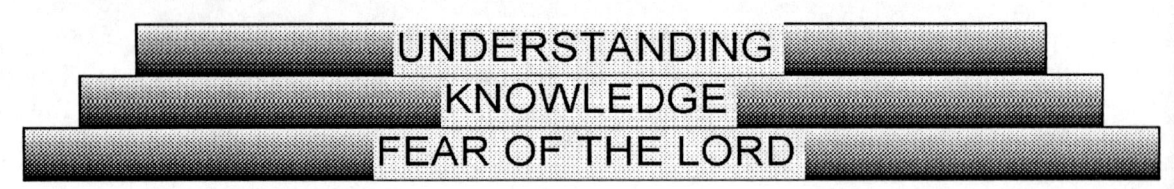

```
        UNDERSTANDING
         KNOWLEDGE
        FEAR OF THE LORD
```

Let's review those same three steps again.

- FEAR = To have awesome reverence for God. Godliness.
- KNOWLEDGE = To learn, accumulate relevant information, and remember (know) them. To begin transforming the mind to right thinking.
- UNDERSTANDING = To have the ability to comprehend (internalize) and fuse together what is known. A total release of our identity comes from understanding the administration of the Word in our life.

You'll notice that often knowing and understanding are paired together. Luke said that the **disciples *understood* nothing that Jesus told them and they didn't *know* the things He told them concerning His death** (Luke 18:34). In other words, they heard and remembered what Jesus said, but it meant nothing.

- We're told to **lean not to our own <u>understanding</u>** (Prov. 3:5), and we know from personal experience that foolish believers do just that. They react to their own understanding. That's why troubles seem so great. None of us want to admit that we're susceptible to this behavior.
- We can <u>understand</u> what the will of the Lord is (Eph. 5:17).
- Paul prayed, **That the eyes of your <u>understanding</u> being enlightened...** (Eph. 1:16:18). Your spirit man receives revelations of divine understanding that is NOT from the intellect. Rather, it's a precise

---

1. 2 Tim 2:6-7NKJV

The Happiness of Finding Wisdom

THE 3RD STEP.
Understanding

comprehension of revelation derived from God. This revelation of understanding gives you insight into the Word of God and it comes alive. It keeps you safe:

SOLOMON ASKED FOR UNDERSTANDING:

Solomon asked God: **Give therefore thy servant an UNDERSTANDING heart to judge thy people, that I may discern between <u>good and bad</u>...** (1 Kings 3:9). Solomon sought to have an understanding heart. That means one that was discerning, one that would listen and respond to what the Spirit says. Solomon didn't ask for riches and honor, but for understanding. It was through understanding that wisdom became manifest.

Proverbs 7 repeatedly says that from childhood, Solomon was given the commandments to treasure and keep so that he might live. Wisdom and understanding were supposed to keep him from the immoral woman (Prov. 7:5). Solomon had great <u>knowledge</u> of the word – he could recite it back to someone... it just didn't change his behavior. Even though he was told to bind it on his fingers and on the tablets of his heart, he refused. He was told (verse 4) to call wisdom his sister (blood relative) and *understanding* his "kinswoman" (the closest of friends).

The purpose of obeying the commands was to keep the builder of the family name ("my Son") safe. Unfortunately, this wise Solomon was later preoccupied with the distracting thoughts of many women. He surrounded himself with 700 concubines and 300 wives. These women were his downfall. At the end of Solomon's life, he finally realized his weakness and wrote in Ecclesiastes 7:26 that only the man who pleases God will escape the woman who is a snare, but the sinner she will ensnare.

- That woman who is the snare is wrong and foolish thinking that keeps us from understanding.
- The longing of our heart must be to obtain the intimacy of understanding. If we apply this concept to our own lives, we see that wisdom keeps us (the pure bride) from whoredoms.

LIVING FOOLISHLY WITHOUT UNDERSTANDING

We need to keep the facts about Solomon's failure in mind while reading about this foolish man in Proverbs. We already learned how the foolish wife didn't KNOW. Now, let's look at this believer who KNEW the word, but he just didn't UNDERSTAND it. Proverbs 7:6-7 (KJV) **For at the window...through my casement** (lattice for air ventilation) **... I discerned...a young man void of UNDERSTANDING...**

The Happiness of Finding Wisdom

THE 3RD STEP
Understanding

- This believer was without understanding.
- That condition caused him to be unable to discern evil intentions coming toward him.
- He did not have the character or courage to resist flattery.

This simple person doesn't do what he knows is right. His foolishness works full-time to sidetrack him. Consequently, he is neutralized and enslaved into living in the flesh. Those uncaptivated thoughts war against the Kingdom of God within. Wicked imaginations imprison him in his mind.

Oh dear. Do not be unwise, but <u>understand</u> what the will of the Lord is…(Eph. 5:17).

This simple man went alone to the house of the strange woman; he was not a doer of the word. (7:8). **Passing** (literally sauntering or "cruisin" – he was looking for trouble!) **along the street near her corner; and he took the path to her house…** He willfully left what he knew was right and went the wrong direction. He knew where she lived, because he undoubtedly had considered visiting her before. This verse says that he "took the path to her house…" without deviation. Once there, she enticed him with her smooth religious sayings and it all made sense to his carnal nature.

This fool escaped the responsibility of discipleship; he was unable to make correct decisions. He was lost in the glow of feelings, discovering delights of this forbidden environment. This sensuous-based interest denied his past years of virtue.

Now we're talking about spiritual adultery here too. Prov. 7:9-10 (KJV) **In the twilight, in the evening** (at the eye of night), **in the black and dark night: and, behold, there met him a woman with the attire of a harlot, and subtle** (crafty) **of heart**. This foolish man sees her with rose-colored glasses. The closer he gets to her place the darker those glasses get, until his spiritual discernment is lost. Darkness falls and thick blackness blinds him to truth. He strains to see the crafty harlot — she knows what she's doing.

Prov. 7:11 (KJV) **She is loud and stubborn; her feet abide not in her house**. She's boisterous, opinionated, and never satisfied. A gad-about. She has a house -- but it will never be a home. She has no sense of family or community. She lives for the moment in wanderlust – looking for a good time. She wanders from church to church finding stupid ones to influence. She has a harlot's heart that tries to convince him to backslide, to prostitute his morals – and to take away guilt.

The Happiness of Finding Wisdom

THE 3RD STEP.
Understanding

Prov. 7:12 (KJV) **Now is she without, now in the streets** (a streetwalker), **and lieth in wait at every corner.** She's everywhere… at the grocery store, and down the block. She's looking for you. An opportunity to backslide may be waiting at every corner.

Continuing with Proverbs 7:13-20: **So she caught him** (with her words), **and kissed him, and with an impudent** (brazen) **face said unto him, I have peace offerings with me; this day have I paid my vows.** The idea of common faith was the pretext she used to lure him inside. (She had prepared a peace offering – which is meat. Most historians say that this was really an offering to cultic idolatry – she was probably a devotee of Aphrodite. At any rate, she had a good supply of meat on hand and it had to be eaten quickly. She poses as a Christian. In fact, she could expound upon the "deep" things of Scriptural nature (meat). She'd say anything to get him. "Today I prayed! This must be God!" She appeased her conscious with offerings; now she's ready to do what ever she wants. On Sunday she went to church and for the rest of the week she lived like hell. You see, my friend, unlawful sex is not God's plan. Foolish and unlawful unions must not continue.

Therefore come I forth to meet thee (you and you alone, but if someone else had come by first – it would have been him) **diligently to seek thy face, and I have found thee** (and I'll teach you what you need to learn. He was persuaded to spend the night with her). **I have decked my bed with coverings of tapestry, with carved works, with fine linen of Egypt** (worldly coverings). **I have perfumed my bed with myrrh, aloes, and cinnamon** (these aromas represent a false anointing. She used every incitement to get this guy — worship, food, and sex until satisfied).

Come, let us take our fill of love until the morning (let's quench our thirst, let us riot with love)**; let us solace ourselves with loves. For the goodman** (her husband) **is not at home, he is gone a long journey: he hath taken a bag of money with him, and will come home at the day appointed** (perhaps when he's spent it all). And Jesus hasn't returned yet either, so there's time for a few more good times.

With her much fair speech (enticing and persuasive words) **she caused him to yield** (she can be polite and articulate)**, with the flattering of her lips she forced him.** (He didn't fight for long.) **He goeth after her straightway, as an ox goeth to the slaughter** (in his stupidity not thinking that he would be killed), or **as a fool to the correction of the stocks; till a dart strike.** But her main purpose is to get him (you) off the mainstream and into compromise.

Through his liver (the liver filters the blood – dilutes the life that is in the Blood of Christ)**; as a bird hastenth to the snare** (what's fun today won't be tomorrow)**, and**

The Happiness of Finding Wisdom

THE 3RD STEP
Understanding

knoweth not that it is for his life. This guy proceeds onward to his fate. He is likened to an unsuspecting animal bounding into a trap -- like a bird waiting to be snared. There's no escape from this ambush to which he seems sadly oblivious. He pays with his life.

Prov. 7:24-27 (KJV): **Hearken unto me now therefore, O ye children and attend to the words of my mouth.** Here our storyteller renews the correct choices to his sons and begs them to pay attention to his words. **Let not thine heart decline to her ways** (it's your choice to go or not go), **go not astray in her paths** (don't pretend to be a Christian like she does – don't learn her ways or go on her paths).

For she hath cast down many wounded: yea, many strong men have been slain by her. This woman wields instantaneous death to her suitors and many great men have been "toppled" by these encounters with her. **Her house is the way to hell, going down to the chambers of death.** All because he was void of UNDERSTANDING.

** Many of us have encountered foolish ideas and foolish people. Write some examples of your experiences.

WE CAN'T JUST HEAR A GOOD SERMON; WE HAVE TO UNDERSTAND IT!

To become successful, we must integrate our lives with understanding. We must change our false beliefs and assumptions. It's the principle of seedtime and harvest, cause and effect. The result of our belief becomes our future. What does that future look like? Ask yourself, what do I anticipate? Lots of times we hope for one thing and work toward another. But, there's no confusion or double mindedness in God. Truth is:

Right fear =
    right knowing =
        right understanding =
            right thoughts & words =
                right feelings and actions =
                    right decisions =
                        right character =
                            right results!

Jesus asked, **Why do you call me, `Lord, Lord,' and do not do what I say?** Then, He makes a comparison of <u>TWO kinds of men</u>. The first man described is one of <u>understanding</u>), **He who comes to me and (#1) hears my words and (#2) puts them into practice.**

The Happiness of Finding Wisdom

THE 3RD STEP.
understanding comes into the soul

He is like a man <u>building a house</u> (his life), **who dug down deep and laid the foundation on rock** (Jesus). **When a flood came, the torrent struck that house but could not shake it, because it was well built.**

(Now here is Jesus' own definition of a foolish man): **But the one who hears my words and does not put them into practice is like a man who built a house** (his life) **on the ground without a foundation. The moment the torrent struck that house, it collapsed and its destruction was complete.** LU.6:46-49NIV If we don't do what the Lord tells us to do, then we have no foundation and cannot build a house that will stand.

> **Oswald Chambers asks this question in his book *"My Utmost for His Highness,"* "Am I willing to let God do in me all that has been made possible by the Atonement? Wisdom pleads with you to go in the way of <u>understanding</u> (Prov. 9). Write how you will respond. **

UNDERSTANDING COMES INTO THE SOUL

It's not enough to have "head knowledge" or mental assent. We must understand what we know. Understanding demands the action of strategic DOING. Even through the mundane routine we begin to DO what is necessary in order to align our lives to Christ's likeness. Because we understand, we DO what must be done. The more we <u>understand</u> --the easier it is to live a happy life. Every revelation can become an internal revolution.

The Psalmist said (47:7), **Sing praises to him with <u>understanding</u>**. Comprehend why DOING praise is important. Like... don't just come late and yawn! Understand what you are doing. Here's another, Ps 49:3 **My mouth shall speak of wisdom; and the meditation of my <u>heart</u> shall be of <u>understanding</u>.** (KJV) We must <u>understand</u> (comprehend, discern, interpret, digest, perceive, grasp, fathom, believe, and realize, and enact) what we know before we can apprehend it.

Wisdom = understanding what you know and then doing it.

As we begin to order our thinking correctly, a cloud the size of a man's hand begins to fill the sky. If we SEE (comprehend) that cloud, then action begins. As we begin to outrun the chariot, our steps hasten into wholeness. This perception is in the mind. We see the cloud (perception) and imagine ourselves running. Then we do it. We're not born with good thoughts, we learn to have them and respond to them. Our emotions can be made to run in line with our stable and mature expectations.

The Happiness of Finding Wisdom

THE 3RD STEP
understanding comes into the soul

FACTS ABOUT UNDERSTANDING.

Prov 2:2 **We must apply our heart to <u>understanding</u>** (NIV).

Prov 13:15 **Good <u>understanding</u> giveth favor...** (KJV).

Job 28:28 **To depart from evil is <u>understanding</u>.**

Prov 9:10 **For the reverence and fear of God are basic to all wisdom. Knowing God results in every other kind of <u>understanding</u>** (TLB).

Prov 16:22 **<u>Understanding</u> is a wellspring of life to him who has it...** (NKJ).

Ps 14:2 **The LORD looked down from heaven upon the children of men, to see if there were any that did <u>understand</u>, and seek God** (KJV).

- Each of us has a limited view; we generally see only the outward appearance (1 Sam. 16:7). We need to understand what is intended, rather than what we assume.

- If we have partial understanding, then we may be misled. The carnal mind can never discern God's truth. If we interpret facts using our reasoning alone, we may not recognize that our conclusions are false. That's where prejudices and pride are derived. Left to ourselves, we can easily create false biases and unrealistic barriers. When we hope in negative information, then eventually, our hope disappears.

- Job 28:28 says that to **shun evil is understanding**. It's in right understanding that we have power to control our lives and understand how we feel. Thoughts and feelings are inseparably lashed together. If we understand why we feel a certain way, then it's possible that we can also control our attitude and behavior.

- Prov 2:6 says that from **God's mouth come knowledge and understanding**. We only obtain these qualities when we communicate with Him. **In creation, God stretched out the heavens by his understanding** (Prov. 3:19).

- The principle of <u>understanding</u> contains definite limits of comprehension. We are able to contain a concept within a frame of reference that can be used.

The Happiness of Finding Wisdom

THE 3RD STEP.
understanding comes into the soul

The Holy Spirit can bring to remembrance only those concepts that we already understand.

SOME THINGS WE MUST UNDERSTAND:
God births His image into the NEW CREATION human that we might comprehend the fellowship of the mystery, which was hidden in God from the beginning of the world… which the church may make known to all… the manifold <u>wisdom</u> of God (Eph. 4:1).

- We have already died, now we must LIVE.
- God hopes that we will walk away from darkness into light and reveal the Christ. We are children of the light (Eph. 5:8). Here is the manifold wisdom of God; we have overcome every temptation.
- We become what we worship. We reflect the image and nature of God.
- Oh the much variegated and multifarious (manifold) wisdom of God, how wonderful it is. God uses virgins (pure ones) to bear His seed that bring life.
- While Abraham looked for the city (Heb. 11:10)– we BECOME that city set on the hill (Matt. 5:14).
- Our individual dwelling places join together to shine forth the light of the SON.
- The united corporate son reveals God.

AN ESSAY
We need to further understand the concept we discussed earlier about Rom 5:10, **For if, when we were God's enemies, we were reconciled to him through the death of his Son, how much more, having been reconciled, shall be saved through his LIFE!** (NIV) As we consider the reality of becoming the NEW CREATION, we begin to comprehend that Jesus shed His untainted BLOOD (the life of the flesh, Lev. 17:11) to ATONE for our sins. We know also that He gave His LIFE (psuche, sinless soul-life) for our salvation (*sozo*, wholeness, Rom. 5:10). We could think of it this way: The blood accomplishes our initial (or positional) atonement from sin. But… it is His LIFE that accomplishes our ongoing progressive *sozo,* that provides wholeness of mind and character.

Somehow, much of the church world stops with the POSITIONAL salvation. Bless God, we went forward down the aisle and confessed our sins — now our duty is over! But we

The Happiness of Finding Wisdom

THE 3RD STEP
understanding comes into the soul

never quite figured out how to "put on the New Man" — or live successfully as a Christian. Well, we might have tried in our excited days of being a new convert and first finding God, but as time went on, we forgot and re-incorporated many of our old ways. Somewhere along the way, "I'm a new creation" became a great song that we now heartily sing without giving much consideration to it's meaning. Funny how the whole church world wants to "go to heaven" without bothering to DO what the Bible says.

Worldly ways still have strong entrance into the heart of the modern church. Many aloof, arrogant, and proud Christians exemplify the fallen self-pleasing nature of self-determination. Others are passively yielding and compliant. Compromise rules the masses of once-committed believers who have now lost their holy boundaries. Much of our "religion" has become extremely worldly. Yet, Paul cautioned us to find another way.

Gal 2:20, **I m crucified with Christ: nevertheless I LIVE; yet not I, but Christ liveth in me: and the life which I now live in the flesh I live by the faith of the Son of God, who loved (*agapao*) me...** (KJV). This means we lose our soulish identity and become a class of people on earth who migrate to the next dimension of LIVING.

<u>"I am crucified with Christ,"</u> Paul explains how this act of being crucified was already accomplished by the blood of the Savior in the initial salvation experience. Through the cross, we become partakers of this promise — we have already been crucified (impaled in company with Christ). It's already done! We don't have to keep dying again and again. We're not like the hero in the old western movies who keeps rising up with "just a flesh wound." Reckon it done (Rom. 6:11). The problem is that we need to stay dead.

But God forbid that I should boast except in the cross of our Lord Jesus Christ, by whom the world has been crucified to me, and I to the world. (NKJ) IT is already done... I am crucified to the world. "They that are Christ's have crucified (already finished) the flesh (Gal. 5:24)." Now, all we have to do is not nurture that OLD MAN nature. It remains dead and buried far away from our present day actions.

<u>"Nevertheless, I LIVE."</u> Understanding imparts the necessity of maintaining death to the old nature. It doesn't haunt me. I become partner in His life! Death is swallowed up in LIFE (1 Cor. 15:54). My work is not to repeatedly crucify myself, live in a convent, or be separated from all monetary influence. My position (as a NEW CREATION) is to maintain the flesh in a crucified state. My evil nature becomes totally separated from my renewed thoughts, my controlled actions, and my disciplined desires. I'm crucified from mySELF." That's how I'm free to inherit God's zoe LIFE. I live (I am quickened by the same spirit that raised Jesus from the dead.)

The Happiness of Finding Wisdom

THE 3RD STEP.
understanding comes into the soul

Just like the angry crowd taunted Jesus on the cross, all my carnal nature and reactions continue to cry out, "Come down from the cross." (Mark 15:30) But, it's my duty to maintain absolute control over the sinful old nature.

<u>"I LIVE."</u> Living happens by allowing the Holy Spirit to conduct His specific job of revealing the NEW CREATION nature in me. He unveils "Christ living in me" — the anointed power to obtain my destiny.

> *Anointing = the enabling power of God given for you to accomplish your purpose.*

<u>"Christ LIVETH in me."</u> No longer will I be satisfied with just knowing the power of the cross to ATONE. Jesus now LIVES (abides) in resurrection power within to cause me to exhibit LIFE — to be like Him in character and nature — to understand the full power of ongoing salvation. Heb 7:25 tells us, "Therefore he is able to SAVE COMPLETELY those who come to God through him, because he ALWAYS LIVES to INTERCEDE for them" NIV. That's how we can LIVE…

<u>"I LIVE by faith</u> in the Son of God." Yes, I LIVE the quickened life – the God-kind of LIFE that comes by faith. That NEW CREATION life comes and DWELLS (abides) in me — right now — here in this lifetime.

Jesus explained it often. John 17:11 says, "Now I am no longer in the world, but these are IN THE WORLD...." (NKJ) Believers remain here living above this (cosmos) worldly system.

John 17:14 "…and the world has hated them because they are NOT OF THE WORLD (world systems), just as I am NOT OF THE WORLD."(NKJ) We are "not of the world, "JUST AS" (Strong's # 2531 *kathos*) Christ is "not of the world." It is out of this likeness to Christ, that we obtain this quality to resist the worldly nature.

Jesus did not pray that we be taken "OUT of the world" (vs.15), or suddenly "raptured" away, but that we be "kept from the evil one." There's no escapism clause here. Believers are to be separated OUT of the old way and that separation is what causes them to be "kept from the evil one." But that's not all. We not just separated OUT, but also are separated INTO the New LIFE. The NEW CREATION human lives IN THIS WORLD while not being OF THE WORLD. That means we no longer endlessly contend with our worldly nature, or are tempted by the carnality of the worldly systems.

The Happiness of Finding Wisdom

THE 3RD STEP
understanding comes into the soul

John 17:16 They are NOT OF THE WORLD, just as I am NOT OF THE WORLD. (NKJ)

- <u>Not of the world.</u> The NEW CREATION manifests the God kind of LIFE that is in Jesus, not that of the world. We demonstrate, as much as possible, a life without sin.

- <u>Not of the world</u>. We walk in the same realm as Jesus ("just as" He was NOT OF THIS WORLD); hence we are just as He is, in His presence.

- <u>Not of the world</u>. We establish God's kingdom on earth as it is in heaven (Matt. 6:10). We belong to a kingdom that is NOT OF THIS WORLD (Jn. 8:23, 18:36). We live independently from this worlds systems, with eternal governing standards and principles.

- <u>Not of the world.</u> We live in the world, in order to "redeem" (salvage) the world, but we are not "of" the world.

Jesus became the first fruit example of "living in the world, but not being part of it." Paul said, **Jesus gave himself to redeem us from all wickedness and to purify for himself a people that are his very own, eager to do what is good.** (Titus 2:14 NIV). Jesus determined to send this redeemed people INTO THE WORLD (John 17:18 NKJ). The NEW CREATION is sent INTO THE WORLD (cosmos/systems), exhibiting a new nature. They walk in covenantal fellowship with God and man. They no longer loose the battle against the flesh; they manifest dominion rule. 1 John 4:17 says, **Herein is our love made perfect, that we may have boldness in the Day of Judgment: because AS HE IS, SO ARE WE --IN THIS WORLD.** (KJV) As He is, we are.

We come as absolute victors into "this world" over which the devil has long ruled as prince. Here, we live above evil influences -- as examples, teaching and warning men in all wisdom, that they might mature in Christ (Col. 2:28). As we SEPARATE from worldly ways, God builds His house in us; He will "receive us" (2 Cor 6:1617). This phenomenal promise remains for those that maintain a NEW CREATION lifestyle... **For... I will dwell in them, and walk in them**... (KJV) Let us make a fresh declaration in accordance with the will of God — from every corner of the earth the "now" purposes of God must be released. We have come to the "set time" (Ps. 102), a time for complete and radical renovation of our current mindset.

Jesus, fully man and fully spirit, became our example of how to live in this earth as a human who resides in the spiritual realm that does not touch "this WORLD." As we imitate Him, we move into this place of no longer DOING, but BEING the demonstration of the power of God (1 Cor. 2:4).

The Happiness of Finding Wisdom

THE 3RD STEP.
understanding comes into the soul

Just think, Jesus came to seek and save <u>that</u> (not *who*) which was lost (Luke 19:10). This verse means that one reason Jesus died was to save (make spiritually whole) our lost carnal minds (from the Fall). We need to have creation minds like *before* the fall – spiritually discerning and knowing. The work of the cross enables us to no longer think like "this world." Our salvation allows God to manifest His glory upon the LIFE we lead.

Notice the interrelated steps again as Isaiah told of a Messiah who would possess all these qualities: **The Spirit of the LORD will rest on him— the Spirit of <u>wisdom</u> and of <u>understanding</u>, the Spirit of counsel and of power, the Spirit of <u>knowledge</u> and of the <u>fear of the LORD</u>— and he will <u>delight in the fear of the LORD</u>.** (Isa. 11: 2 NIV).

- Jer 3:15 **Then I will give you shepherds** (pastors) **after my own heart** (filled with awesome reverence)**, who will lead you with <u>knowledge and understanding</u>.** NIV

The effective functioning interplay of these steps (above) thrusts the believer toward the purposes of God which have so far been undisclosed. As we bring forth these unhindered qualities, we become custodians of our own destiny and that of the earth.

ALL THREE

These concepts all interrelate. In order to be wise, we move up and down over these <u>three interconnected</u> steps of fear, knowing, and understanding.

Prov. 2:1-5 **My son** (the heir or builder of the family name)**,**
If thou wilt (you have individual choice to cooperate)
Receive my words (sayings that provide salvation)
And hide (lay up in a safe place to use later)
My commandments with thee; (the Divine promise is conditional)

So that thou incline (lean toward to bid welcome)
Thine ear unto wisdom, (not just listen with ears but receive in heart)
And apply thine heart to <u>understanding</u> (receive the word with readiness of mind)

Yea, if thou search after knowledge (know the worth of it and pant after it.
And liftest up thy voice for <u>understanding</u>; (submit your voice and call out for it)

The Happiness of Finding Wisdom

THE 3RD STEP
understanding comes into the soul

If thou seekest her as silver (search for redemption as a hidden treasure, preferring it above the wealth of the world).
And searchest for her as hid treasures (that which can be found);
Then shalt thou <u>understand</u> the <u>fear</u> of the Lord, (that is, you shall learn how to reverence and worship Yahweh, and be led into the meaning and mystery of His purposes).
And find the <u>knowledge</u> of Eloheim. (It is our interest to know God).
by agreeable affections towards him and adorations of him). Notice our three steps again!

For <u>wisdom</u> will enter your heart, (His free gift and He gives it liberally James 1:7).
And <u>knowledge</u> will be pleasant to your soul...(bring happiness)
And <u>understanding</u> will guard you (and you'll know how to conduct yourselves in all situations and toward all people) (Prov 2:10-11 NIV).[1]

        1. Fear, the reverence of Truth
        2. Knowledge, the learning of Truth
        3. Understanding, the correct interpretation of Truth
        _____
        = Wisdom, the application of Truth

---

[1]. Some definitions from Matthew Henry's Commentary on the Whole Bible: New Modern Edition, Electronic Database. Copyright (c) 1991 by Hendrickson Publishers, Inc.

The Happiness of Finding Wisdom

7 THE PILLARS OF WISDOM:

THE STRUCTURE OF THE HOUSE

My life is a temple of God and I am a wise wife. I arise and build.
(1 Chron. 22:19, Neh. 2:20).

Most of us have long searched for that place of connection -- that supernatural "happening" -- that mighty demonstration of miracles -- forgetting that His very Kingdom is within us. We have looked outside toward every traveling big name to usher us into a place of excitement and new phenomenon. But, we've forgotten that Truth (like that still small voice) resides within. While we expect God to come down or suddenly "appear" to do something – We forget that He's arising from within and pressing the inner person outward.

We've been learning from Lady Wisdom about building our house. Because we contain His precious presence, we must carefully build the enclosure for His residence in the Most Holy Place of our Temple – in the precious inner sanctuary. It's the place where we passed through the shrouded veil into the place where the cherubim's wings touch … where we come face to face with God. It's the place where we become whole. It's where we've integrated with God's nature and come into unity with His desires. It's there that He arises. Let God arise (Ps. 68:1)! Believers contain (embody) that arising presence within themselves. In other words, God occupies our temple. Wisdom builds the HOUSE for Emanuel's nature (the God with us and in us).

Our definition of wisdom continues to unfold = the state of containing and participating in God's active presence. Wisdom is the process of enlightened building and vitalized living. God says to get it (Prov. 4:5). Make Wisdom the most important thing (Prov. 4:7). Be anxious for it. You can't live without it. Receive it zealously. Get it.

Exalt her (wisdom)**, and she** (wisdom) **shall promote** (to advance in rank, or position) **thee; she shall bring thee to honor** (elevate in honor, character, and quality)**, when thou dost embrace** (to receive gladly) **her.** (Prov. 4:8 KJV).

THE 7 PILLARS:

I was reading Proverbs 9 while on a recent trip to India. I'd probably read it at least a

7 THE PILLARS OF WISDOM:
THE STRUCTURE OF THE HOUSE

hundred times before – but suddenly it made sense and explained itself. Our house can't stand unless each pillar solidly supports the structure. These necessary pillars are explained within these verses! They are separate and distinct activities that must combine in strength to uphold our structure. And from this understanding – this book was built.

Returning to our text Scripture (Prov. 9:1-3).

> *Wisdom has built her house. She has hewn out her <u>seven pillars</u>.*
> *She has slaughtered her meat. She has mixed her wine,*
> *She has also furnished her table. She has sent out her maidens,*
> *She cries out from the highest places of the city.*

The word "pillar" means something set upright and stationed to establish boundaries. In ancient times, pillars held up the rest of the building and the roof. They were usually quarried out of marble and were often the only things left standing through the centuries.

> There are pillars of the earth (Job 9:6, Ps. 75:3) and pillars of heaven (Job 26:11).
>
> Rev. 3:12, "If you conquer, I will make you a pillar in the temple of my God; you will never go out of it. i will write on you the name of my God, and the name of the city of my God, the new Jerusalem that comes down from my God out of heaven..." Gensenius translates this verse, "I will assign him a firm and abiding place in the everlasting kingdom of God."

7

Seven, of course, represents the number of perfection -- the fullness of the Spirit, seven golden candlesticks, seven all-powerful horns, seven all-seeing eyes. There are seven creation days, seven colors in the rainbow, and seven colors on Joseph's coat all revealing the far reaching nature of the overcomer. We forgive 70x7. The Jericho walk was seven times. The ram's horns of Jubilee blow seven times, etc.

> Lady Wisdom's seven pillars are built on the three-step foundation we discussed earlier: the Fear of the Lord, Knowledge, and Understanding.

The Happiness of Finding Wisdom

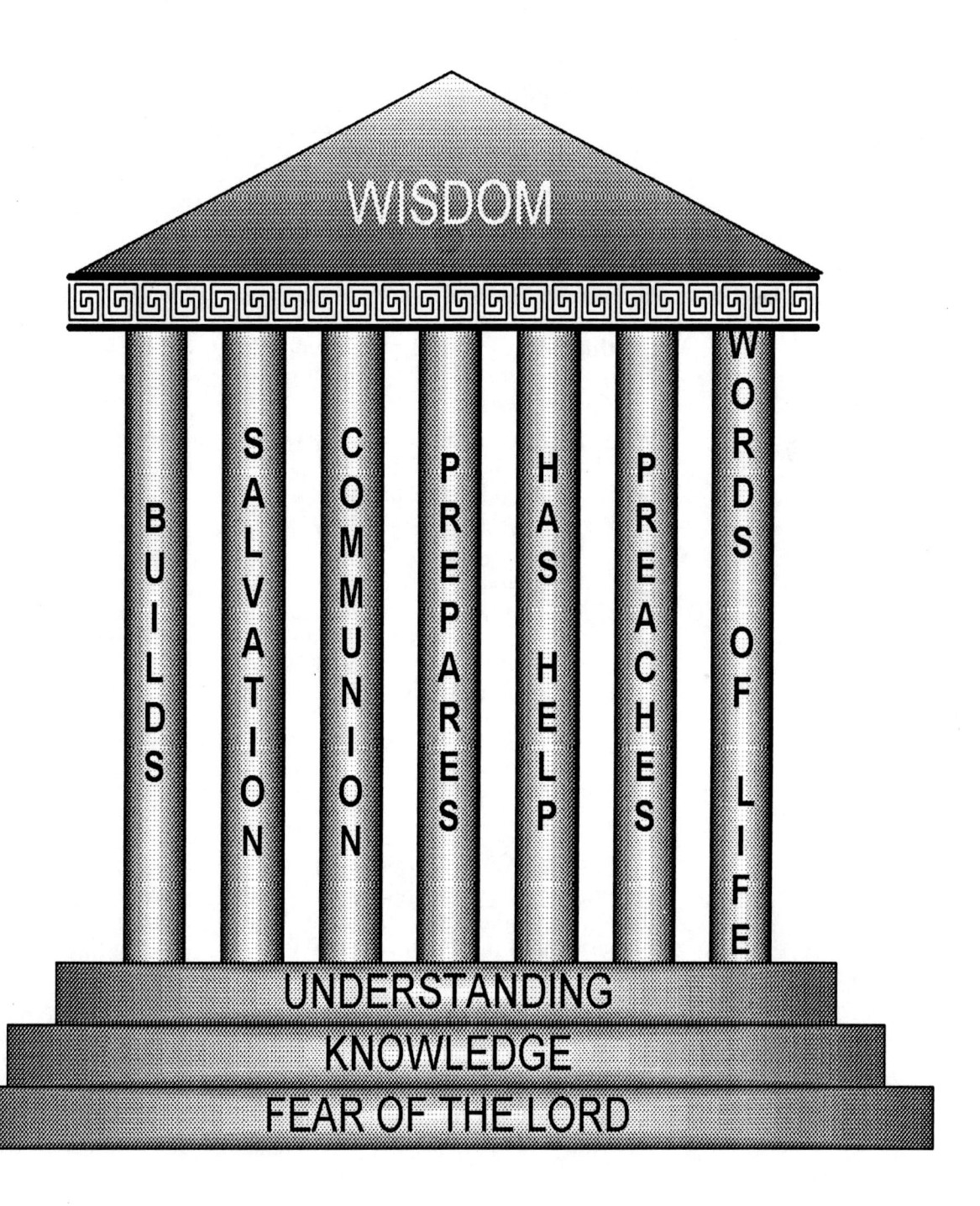

7 THE PILLARS OF WISDOM:
THE STRUCTURE OF THE HOUSE

WISDOM

- BUILDS
- SALVATION
- COMMUNION
- PREPARES
- HAS HELP
- PREACHES
- WORDS OF LIFE

UNDERSTANDING
KNOWLEDGE
FEAR OF THE LORD

The Happiness of Finding Wisdom　　　　6-99

7 THE PILLARS OF WISDOM:
THE STRUCTURE OF THE HOUSE

ONE

The first pillar of wisdom's temple clearly stands out as the mere fact that <u>she built according to a purposeful plan</u>. This building requires her purposeful effort to accomplish an end result, but the floor plan is not her own design. We see this principle again in Prov 14:1, **"Every wise woman buildeth her house: but the foolish plucketh it down with her hands"** (KJV).

You need a God kind of plan. Paul spoke of visiting the Corinthians, **"Therefore, when I was planning this, did I do it carefully? Or the things I plan, do I plan according to the flesh…"** (Prov. 1:16 NKJ). Did you find that blueprint plan of your great Architect?

TWO

We'll call the **second pillar "Salvation:"** in other words, "Wisdom slaughtered her meat." She killed the old nature and received the sacrificial lamb for salvation.

In the New Testament, Jesus explains the significance of the particular action signified in this column (Matthew 22:1-4), "The kingdom of heaven <u>is like</u> a certain king who arranged a marriage for his son, and sent out his servants to call those who were invited to the wedding; and they were not willing to come. (Luke 14:23 says, "Go out into the highways and hedges and compel them to come in, that my house may be filled.) Again, he sent out other servants, saying, `tell those who are invited, "see, <u>I have prepared my dinner</u>; <u>my oxen and fatted cattle are killed</u>, <u>and all things are ready</u>. Come to the wedding.'" (NKJ).

The sacrifice of the perfect lamb was completed and Wisdom made the dinner. Now, there's meat in the Father's house. Wisdom diligently worked and the great wedding supper is finished. The preparation of meat is for the end time.

THREE

We'll call the **third pillar** "Bread and Wine" or **<u>Communion</u>**. We hear Wisdom refer to this action when she says, (Prov 9:5) **"Come, eat of my <u>bread</u> and drink of the <u>wine</u> I have mixed."** Lady Wisdom had <u>bread</u> to share with others. The emblems of the body of Jesus represents the death of the Son of Man, the sacrificed Humanity that purchased our healing and soul realm wholeness.

The Happiness of Finding Wisdom

John 6:48 **I am that <u>bread</u> of LIFE.** (KJV)

John 6:51 **I am the LIVING <u>bread</u> which came down from heaven: if any man eat of this bread, he shall live forever: and the bread that I will give is my flesh, which I will give for the LIFE of the world** (KJV).

John 6:58 …. **He that eateth of this <u>bread</u> shall LIVE forever.**

The second part of this column is: "**She mixed her <u>wine</u>.**" Some renditions say that she mingled wine with honey and spices. The Greek LXX translation interprets this portion as, "She has mingled her wine in a bowl." Revelation 14:10 explains that the wicked will drink the wine of God's wrath *unmixed*. From that, we deduce that the believer will drink mixed or mingled wine.

Of course, Wisdom's wine spoke of the sacrificial blood that was shed by the Son of God, the Deity that took away sin. Jesus gave this perfect sacrifice of His blood), so that we could become LIKE HIM. As we partake of His flesh and blood it demonstrates our reception of that LIFE. Communion is a sharing of LIFE that includes all that He is and all that we are.

Wisdom's well-planned life allowed her to intimately know of the sacrifice that was to come. Her own preparation spoke of Jesus. She made the bread and mingled the wine — she didn't use someone else's revelation. Wisdom cooked the bread of life (His body) – until that revelation became her own — and now she shared it with others. She mixed the wine, while understanding and appropriating this symbolic representation into eternal revelation for the lives of others. Wisdom <u>mingled</u> and mixed the regenerative activity of the bread and wine into every area of life.

Luke 22:19-20, **"This is my body (bread) which is given for you, do this in remembrance of me…. The cup (wine) is the covenant in my blood which is shed for you."** Wisdom understood the full relationship of communion for salvation and healing. She offered that deep understanding to others.

7 THE PILLARS OF WISDOM:
THE STRUCTURE OF THE HOUSE

FOUR

Pillar 4: Wisdom sets the table. She PREPARES and is attentive to details. Not only did she make dinner, and have the communion ready— then she made the table appear attractive. She "furnished" or set it in order. Sometimes when company comes over, I really like to make a flower arrangement. Then, I get out the good plates and a few candles. After all that fussing, it seems like the food tastes better.

It's called excellence. Wisdom prepared a full and festive feast. It was a communion table with the flesh and blood of His body and the wine that was His blood. She makes her surroundings ready for the big event. Notice how she not only cooked and brought in the unlovable, but she made certain that everything looked good. The guests find this presentation attractive. We have to fix up the table for those that we try to impact. It takes effort and some hospitality to exhibit the abundance of all that God offers.

FIVE

Pillar five. She sends women. SHE HAS HELP. This passage illustrates how wisdom has covenant relationships with others. This word for 'women' can mean young people either male or female. In Eastern custom, an invitation to a banquet (Mt. 22:3) was usually sent by a company of females that was proceeded by eunuchs. Wisdom sent these messengers from door to door to find those who lack understanding. Their message was to forsake foolishness and get understanding. Notice that these people worked cooperatively together. In other words, no Lone Ranger(s). In the many-membered bride, you and I can corporately take our place.

OUR RELATIONSHIPS with others: We live in an instant society… and want everything right now. We enjoy food in seconds, tax refunds on same day we file, and we rarely have to wait for anything. But, one eternal principle is not instant — that of covenant relationship with one another. We must have that vertical relationship with God and then develop that horizontal relationship with each other. God is a covenant God Who only relates to us in terms of covenant. The image and likeness of God's covenantal concept must spread into all areas of our lives.

Apostolic ministry ushers the present-day church into the necessity of re-establishing accurate covenantal relationship – those that don't change because of circumstance. We are to become a covenantal company. We are to lose our present soulish identity and

The Happiness of Finding Wisdom

7 THE PILLARS OF WISDOM:
THE STRUCTURE OF THE HOUSE

become a class of people on earth who issue the clarion cry for unity. That's difficult in these days of disappointing association.

Only time can prove the validity of personal covenant with another human. Surely, the journey in Christian relationship won't be traveled in a few months of weekly meetings. Yet, building covenant relations is a vital factor. We need to expand and elevate our vision — stop thinking individually and start thinking globally.

The proclamation of unity is issued, and the Spirit stirs up those whose great exploits bring Majestic intervention into this present reality. We can't journey this trip of salvation alone. We are joint *heirs together* (Rom. 8:17) in our blessed future. God is "Our Father," and "Christ *in us* (plural)" is the hope of glory. We are to become that "company of saints," a many-membered composite bride. Together.

The word <u>glory</u> means "heavy weight." We're not supposed to count our flocks; we're to weigh them! There's no easy way to maturity and yet the crux of divinity waits for us to learn covenant relationships. We are not called to grow a church – we're called to grow up! Together.

You're not alone. Jesus also experienced disappointing relationships. When Jesus was at the cross, the chosen apostles barred themselves in a locked room. Meanwhile, left nearly alone, the church was born out of His side. Once, 5000 left him in a day. Yet, He died that we might learn differently. The assignment of maturity is upon us... hear him talk to you? We need to stand with one another and not break our alliances because of misfortunate circumstances.

We must move from legalism to Kingdom love. It isn't easy to love without expectation of reward. For surely, beloved, you will be disappointed again and again. Luke 21:16-19 reminds us: "**<u>You will</u> be betrayed even by parents, brothers, relatives and friends, and <u>they will</u> put some of you to death. All <u>men will</u> hate you because of me... <u>by standing firm</u> you will gain life**" NIV.

We know that we have passed from death to life (1 Jn. 3:14), when we have love for the brethren. In other words, that NEW CREATION doesn't wear its feelings on the sleeve. Others no longer wear us out. Relationships are no longer altered or impacted by what others say or think. Jesus is coming back for church that stands together firmly in victory and that walks *together* in the spirit. Let us migrate to the next level of indefatigable persistence toward covenant relationships. Let's breakthrough with new revelation and expectation.

The Happiness of Finding Wisdom

7 THE PILLARS OF WISDOM:
THE STRUCTURE OF THE HOUSE

Faithfulness is a fruit of spirit — defined as "committed, trustworthy, loyal, reliable, constant, steadfastness, & sincere." Faithfulness & commitment are demonstrated thorough a performance of duty, or keeping ones word or promises to one to whom you are loyal. That means you keep your promises regardless of any change or disappointment that might occur.

A complete and radical renovation of our current mindset will position us into actually participating TOGETHER in God's end time plan. Let us embrace this dynamic new experience of enjoying trusted relationships. Let's embrace the vital necessity to corporately progress in our spiritual journey. **"Yes, the set time has come... for He shall appear in His glory. This will be written of the generation to come..."** (And that's us! Ps. 102)

Transformation requires an expanded vision beyond our limited self-centered perceptions. Let us make a fresh prophetic declaration in accordance with the will of God. From every corner of the earth the "now" purposes of God must be released. The point being, Wisdom uses whosoever wants to work (vs. 3), and many want to helper. Joel explains that both women and men, old and young will be a part of the endtime harvest.

SIX

Pillar 6. Wisdom <u>preaches in the high places</u>, always in the manifest presence of God. Proverbs 8 tells more about what she says.

- Hearken unto me for blessed are they that keep her ways (vs. 32).
- Hear my instruction, be wise, and refuse it not (33).
- Watch daily and wait at the post of my door (34).
- Don't sin against me; it's a sin against your own soul (35).
- If you don't love wisdom, you love death (vs. 31-36).

THE HIGH PLACE: She cries out in places of government and dominion. Even her house situates itself at the top of the hill (in Mt Zion). Prov 15:24 says that **the road of the Godly leads <u>upward</u>, leaving hell behind**. We see wisdom <u>standing</u> in that high place, (Prov 8:1-2) preaching as follows: **"Doth not wisdom cry? ... She standeth in the top of <u>high places</u>** (places of vantage, on a hilltop, or Zion. She stands there in God's presence leading the foolish to understanding), **by the way in the places** (finding them in their crises in life) **of the paths** (where things happen, the crossroads). A few examples of "High places" as used in this context follow:

The Happiness of Finding Wisdom

7 THE PILLARS OF WISDOM:
THE STRUCTURE OF THE HOUSE

Job 25:2 …**He maketh peace in his <u>high places</u>.** (KJV)

Ps 18:33 **He maketh my feet like hinds' feet, and setteth me upon my <u>high places</u>.** (KJV)

Isaiah 58:14 **Then shalt thou delight thyself in the LORD; and I will cause thee to ride upon the <u>high places</u> of the earth, and feed thee with the heritage of Jacob** …(KJV)

SEVEN

Pillar seven: <u>Her words give life</u>. So many Christians use poorly chosen words to speak death, partiality, and judgment. Her message (vs.5) to all was, **"Come, eat."** There's enough to feed them all.

Wisdom's words cry out a six-fold invitation:
- Turn in hither
- Come eat
- Come drink
- Forsake foolishness
- Live
- Go in the way of <u>understanding</u>

She entreats, Prov. 8:5 **O ye simple, <u>understand</u> wisdom: and, ye fools, be ye of an <u>understanding</u> heart.** (KJV) That's because her life has been radically changed. Her healed mind speaks encouraging words of life. She says, **"Come eat of my bread** (word of God that she has understood), **and drink of wine which I have mingled** (learn what the blood has done – see how it works in my life!). **Forsake foolishness and live, go in the way of understanding** (walk in the way of insight) RSV.

We'll discover that the Wise bride sees the overall picture. She decides to build according to the plan (blueprint). She decides to stand and not sit, to preach (cry out) and not call, to work and not wait. She probably doesn't know the whole plan at first – but discerns it as she goes along.

The Happiness of Finding Wisdom

7 THE PILLARS OF WISDOM:
THE STRUCTURE OF THE HOUSE

In contrast, the foolish woman (harlot, carnal Christian) <u>sits near the high place</u>, almost at the right place, and says, (Prov 9:17) **Stolen water is sweet, and bread eaten in secret is pleasant.** This fool has no wine (wine speaks of the blood of Christ and the Holy Spirit); she only has water that isn't even hers (stolen). She has no personal testimony because she has always taken the bread and eaten it secretly. She's never learned to work, to study, or to pray. Her words are empty and just sound like what others might preach. The foolish woman's words are death to all who visit, while Wisdom's words are life and instruction.

Wisdom's words	Harlot's words
Truthfullness	Coarse jesting and foolishness
Sincere	Mischievous
Life-giving	Deceptive

Write about how your choice of words relates to the obtaining the wisdom of God. Then in your own words, re-write John 17:17, Proverbs 8:6-8 (AMP) and what Jesus said in Matthew 12:35-37 (AMP).

For we all often stumble and fall and offend in many things.
And if anyone does not offend in speech – never says the wrong things –
he is a fully developed character and a perfect man,
able to control his whole body and curb his entire nature.
James 3:2 Amp.

A REVIEW OF WISDOM'S DINNER:

Wisdom made lavish preparations for all those that will be disciples. This is probably where our Savior borrowed those parables in which He compared the kingdom of heaven to a great supper (Matt 22:2; Luke 14:16).

Not finding a house spacious enough for all her guests, Wisdom intentionally builds a substantial and grand building with seven pillars. She has moved past the legalistic church age and into the love of God and the love of humanity. Here she presents a splendid, sumptuous, but sacred feast, likened to the sacrifice that Christ offered of Himself for us. It is also similar to the feast that Ahasuerus made to show the riches of his glori-

7 THE PILLARS OF WISDOM:
THE STRUCTURE OF THE HOUSE

ous kingdom. Likewise, Isaiah spoke of that meal so long ago (25:6), **On this mountain the LORD Almighty will prepare a feast of rich food for all peoples, a banquet of aged wine— the best of meats and the finest of wine** (NIV).

- Observe that it is all Wisdom's own doing: she has killed the beasts, she has mingled the wine and with her own hands has made excellent preparations. We noticed also that the grace of the gospel is set beautifully as a representation of the Lord's Supper (His body and blood).

- The invitation Wisdom gives is not to some particular friends, but to all in general; that they would come and take part of these abundant provisions.

- Wisdom <u>stands</u> with the invitation. Notice the similarity in John 7:37, **On the last and greatest day of the Feast, Jesus <u>stood</u> and said in a loud voice, "If anyone is thirsty, let him come to me and drink."** NIV

- Likewise, Wisdom cries upon the highest places of the city, as one earnestly desirous of the welfare of the children of men, and grieves to see them rejecting truth.

Now, let's see to whom the invitation is given:

- **Whoso is simple, v. 4** If we were to have a party we would probably want to seek out the philosophers and famous people, that we might hear their wisdom. But our lady friend, Wisdom, invited the down and outer, because what she has to give is what they most need.

- **Whoso ... wants understanding**. Those invited wanted to change and develop understanding. Wisdom's preparations were designed for the most valuable cure ... that of the understanding mind.

- **Whosoever he be**. The invitation is general, and excludes none that don't exclude themselves. They shall be welcome. **Jesus came not to call the righteous, but sinners, not the wise in their own eyes, who say they see** (John 9:41). The call is to those that are willing to become foolish, that they might become wise (1 Cor 3:18).

Look at what the invitation entails:

The Happiness of Finding Wisdom

7 THE PILLARS OF WISDOM:
THE STRUCTURE OF THE HOUSE

- An invitation to her (Wisdom's) house: **Turn in hither.** Is there anyone reading this book who doesn't need to heed that invitation to obtain understanding? Wisdom desires to have deep conversation with us.

- We are invited to eat from her table (v. 5): **Come, eat of my bread,** that is, taste of the true pleasures that are to be found in the "Fear of the Lord," and the knowledge of Who He is. She says, "Taste of the communion that I have found." Wisdom calls those who by faith will act on the Gospel promises, apply them personally, and take nourishment from them. We are to feed and feast upon the provisions that Christ has provided. And, so it is in the spiritual world, what we eat and drink becomes incorporated into our nature and we become refreshed by that understanding.

What is required of those that may have the benefit of this invitation?

- They must break off from all bad relationships: **"Forsake the foolish, converse not with them, conform not to their ways, have no fellowship with the works of darkness, or with those that deal in such works"** (vs. 6). Wisdom departs from evildoers – and so must we.

- Next, they are told to awake and arise from the dead; and live. **"Live not a mere animal-life, as brutes, but now, at length, live the life of men. Live and you shall live; live spiritually, and you shall live eternally"** (Eph 5:14).

- They must choose the paths of Wisdom, and "keep to them with right reason." It's not enough to forsake the foolish, but they must join with others that walk in wisdom; walking in the same spirit and steps.

Wisdom instructs her maidens (pure ones) about their work:

- Not only to search for souls, or to give a general offer for salvation, but also they must address certain people with the unusual message of reproof and rebuke, v. 7, 8.

- Without hesitation, they must instruct these certain ones on how to live more correctly, v. 9.

- The Word of God brings reproof, correction, and instruction in righteousness (2 Tim. 3:16).

The Happiness of Finding Wisdom

7 THE PILLARS OF WISDOM:
THE STRUCTURE OF THE HOUSE

What different sorts of people will these messengers encounter, and how should they respond to them? What success might they expect?

- They would meet with some <u>scorners</u> and wicked men who would mock the messengers of the Lord, misuse them, and would laugh them to scorn. (See also 2 Chron. 30:10, Matt 22:6).

- They are advised to not rebuke the scorner. **Reprove not a scorner; cast not these pearls before swine,** Matt 7:6. Thus Christ said of the Pharisees, **Let them alone**, Matt 15:14. "**Do not reprove them.**"

- Scorners have forfeited their favor. **Those that are thus filthy, let them be filthy still; those that are joined to idols, let them alone**...(Rev. 22:11).

- Why do we leave them alone? Firstly, you waste time and just get disappointed. Those kind of people rarely change. Secondly, you exasperate them and they will hate you and accuse you falsely. Therefore you had better not meddle with them, for your reproofs will be likely to do more hurt than good.

Thankfully, all are not scorners.

- We'll also meet with some who are wise for themselves (I call them legends in their own mind). If this happens, we should *reprove* them. Reprove doesn't mean to "bawl out," but to speak the Word of God more correctly to them, as Priscilla and Aquila spoke to Apollos (Acts 18:26). Some smart men often think that their wisdom exempts them from reproof ... but really, the more wisdom a person has, the more desirous he should be to have his weaknesses shown him.

- In giving our admonitions (corrections), we must also give instructional teaching (v. 9). We should expect that our correction will be taken as a kindness. Ps 141:5 says that a wise man assumes that his friends will deal faithfully with him: **Rebuke such a one, and he will love thee for thy plain dealing, will thank thee, and desire thee to do him the same good turn another time, if there be occasion**. It equally important for Wisdom to take a reproof as well as to give it.

- A wise man will increase in wisdom by implementing the instructions given to him; he will grow in knowledge, and increase in grace. None should regard themselves as so good that they don't need to get better.

The Happiness of Finding Wisdom

7 THE PILLARS OF WISDOM:
THE STRUCTURE OF THE HOUSE

>Give him occasion (so says the Septuagint), to show his wisdom, and he will show it, and the acts of wisdom will strengthen the habits.

The instructions Wisdom gives to her maidens for those invited.
- Communicate with the guest what true wisdom is and how to get it. Teach them the first beginnings of wisdom, about the <u>fear of God</u> –a reverence of God's majesty, and a dread of his wrath.
- Fill their mind with the <u>knowledge</u> of the Word of God and the commands that pertain to the service of God (those are called holy things).
- Lead them to <u>understanding</u>. Matt 7:6. **Or the knowledge which holy men have, which was taught by the holy prophets, of those things which holy men spoke as they were moved by the holy Ghost, this is <u>understanding</u>; it is the best and most useful <u>understanding</u>, will stand us in most stead and turn to the best account.**
- Teach them the advantages of wisdom (Prov. 9: 11): **By me thy days shall be multiplied. It will contribute to the health of thy body, and so the years of thy life on earth shall be increased, while men's folly and intemperance shorten their days. It will bring thee to heaven, and there thy days shall be multiplied in infinitum to infinity, and the years of thy life shall be increased without end.**
- Let them know the consequence of their refusing this offer, vs. 12. **If thou be wise, thou shalt be wise for thyself; thou wilt be the gainer by it, not Wisdom.** (Luke 16:12), **but thou shalt carry it** (carnal wisdom) **with thee into another world.**[1]

Later, we hear the Lord summon every believer to another banquet, **Blessed are those who are called to the marriage supper of the Lamb!** (Rev. 19:9 NKJ).

1. Yes, it's not just any feast, it's time to go to the celebration of the wedding.
2. The adolescent bride has matured; she is ready for an intimate relationship.
3. It's time to live the married life!
4. It's time to give life to the seed in this lifetime.

---

1. Some formation of this outline from Matthew Henry's Commentary, ibid.

The Happiness of Finding Wisdom

7 THE PILLARS OF WISDOM:
THE STRUCTURE OF THE HOUSE

Wisdom's 7 Pillars	Foolish woman's 7 pillars
She builds	She is clamorous
She stands	She sits
She has salvation (meat)	She knows nothing
She presents communion	She steals water & hides bread
She makes preparation (sets table)	She waits
She uses others	She sits alone
She stands in high places to preach	She sits near the high place to talk
Her words give life.	Her words are death

What differences! Wisdom preaches what she knows to be true. The foolish steal what others have discovered (stolen bread). In order to be discerning, every believer needs to be able to recognize the various kinds of wisdom.

Wisdom = living by divine concepts!

The Happiness of Finding Wisdom

7 THE PILLARS OF WISDOM:
THE STRUCTURE OF THE HOUSE

THE KINDS OF WISDOM

FINDING THE CORRECT WISDOM

The devil's wisdom:

    The King of Tyre (a picture of the enemy) possessed great wisdom, but he corrupted it. God told him, **You were the model of perfection, full of <u>wisdom</u> and perfect in beauty... and you corrupted** (spoiled, ruined, marred) **your <u>wisdom</u> because of your splendor** (authority, dignity). **So I threw you to the earth...** (Ezek. 28:11-14 NIV). From this Scripture, we understand that God requires non-corrupted wisdom.

The wisdom of Jesus:

    Fallen humanity continues to delve into the depths of the intellect trying to become wise. But, true wisdom is embodied by Jesus. Isaiah 28:29 says, **...The LORD Almighty, wonderful in counsel and magnificent in <u>wisdom</u>** (NIV). Colossians 2:3 tells us that God's wisdom in bound up in Jesus, **In whom are hid all the treasures of <u>wisdom and knowledge</u>** (1 Cor. 1:30). **But of him are ye in Christ Jesus, who of God <u>is made unto us wisdom</u>...** (Col. 2:3). <u>Wisdom is the quality of the Person</u> Who created everything (Prov. 8:22-29). He prepared the heavens and to this day holds the world together.

Man's wisdom & the world's wisdom:

    The Apostle Paul preached about wisdom. He declared that to those who believe, the foolishness of the cross is the <u>wisdom of God</u>. Against the wisdom of God Paul contrasted "the <u>wisdom of this world</u>" (cosmos systems). 1 Cor 1:20 says, **Where is the wise? ... Hath not God made foolish the wisdom of this world?** (KJV) Nothing from God has ever come into the heart of man through his carnal reasoning. (Cor 3:19) **For the <u>wisdom of this world</u> is foolishness with God. For it is written, He taketh the wise in their own craftiness** (KJV).

THE KINDS OF WISDOM
Finding the correct wisdom

- Worldly wisdom often distracts or diverts us with foolishness talk and complacent activities.

- We must believe that for us, the world system is passing away and we have been promoted to a new way of living.

- Paul warns about this "human wisdom," 1 Cor 2:4, **And my speech and my preaching was not with enticing words of man's wisdom, but in demonstration of the Spirit and of power** (KJV). It's not head knowledge or our convincing manner.

- Human wisdom is self-imposed. Often it has no value, but is an indulgence of the flesh that only appears wise (Col. 2:23).

- Human wisdom causes conceit and the pride of life. It keeps us from getting things done, keeps us from doing what is right. It often hinders discerning and proper values.

- True wisdom resists wrong alliances and ungodly belief systems.

1 Cor. 2:5 **That your faith should not stand in the wisdom of men, but in the power of God.** 1 Cor. 2:13-16 **Which things also we speak, not in the words which man's wisdom teacheth…** Wisdom is not how many degrees we have earned, but rather how well we live the life that God intended.

Men's wisdom results in building their own empires, living off ultra spiritual premonitions, reacting jealously, and flattering one another to gain advantage.

Wisdom of this world:

1 Cor 2:6-8 **Howbeit we speak wisdom among them that are perfect** (mature)**: yet not the wisdom of this world** (carnal knowledge. The Biblical view differs with the classical view of wisdom, which sought through reasoned doctrine and rational thought to uncover the mysteries of existence) **nor of the princes** (rulers — important people) **of this world** (cosmos, world systems)**, that come to naught** (have no lasting results).

Paul said, "We speak… to those who are mature." Consequently, we understand that wisdom is not discerned with the natural mind, but it can be expressed to the mature (perfect). Wisdom comes as a

The Happiness of Finding Wisdom

THE KINDS OF WISDOM.
Finding the correct wisdom

revelation to the spiritually minded through His Spirit (vs. 10). The spiritually minded will have an understanding and knowing of truth. God's wisdom is given to us, and now... vs. 16b, we have the mind of Christ. (KJV) We have it.

God's secret wisdom.

1 Cor 2:7-10 **We speak of God's <u>secret</u> (hidden) <u>wisdom</u>, a wisdom that has been hidden and that God destined for our glory before time began** (The Amplified version says, "to lift us into the glory of His presence"). **None of the rulers of this age understood it... no mind has conceived what God has prepared for those who love him"— but God has revealed it** (the secret wisdom) **to us by his Spirit** NIV. We know that wisdom is hidden from rulers of this age – and from demonic forces. But God reveals it to those who seek His character with great resolve.

- "We speak." We speak not with what we learned but with what has been revealed. The NEW CREATION is enabled to concisely verbalize that hidden wisdom with articulate vocabulary that unveils and releases the energy of God's power. With clarity, we can define the process of what needs to be spiritually understood. We speak simply, but with absolute significance.

Spiritual wisdom.

But which the Holy Ghost teacheth; comparing spiritual things with spiritual. But the NATURAL man receiveth <u>not</u> the things of the Spirit of God: A relevant principle of Godly wisdom is that mankind must realize that only God has Truth. God hides it and expects us to get find it and express it.

Think of this, the author of the Bible lives in you! If a famous preacher came to stay at your place, wouldn't you ask him to teach you all the things he had discovered? Wouldn't you ask questions? Well, you need the Holy Spirit to lead you to all Wisdom. Upon the rock of revelation, Christ BUILDS His church in you and me (Matt.16: 13 -19).

- Wisdom produces <u>peaceful treaties</u> with those who oppose (1 Kings. 5:13).

THE KINDS OF WISDOM
Finding the correct wisdom

- The wise know how to conduct their life (Is. 40:20).
- The wise are experts in good living (1 Chron. 22:15).
- The wise son directs life (Prov. 101:1-10).
- Deuteronomy 4:5-10 describes further properties. Wisdom is observable by the nations; you can take possession of the land when you rightly use decrees. **See, I have taught you <u>decrees</u> and laws ... so that you may follow them in the land you are entering to take possession of it. 6) Observe** (condition) **them carefully, <u>for this will show your wisdom and understanding</u> to the <u>nations</u> ...9) Only be careful** (condition)**, and watch yourselves closely** (condition) **so that you do not forget** (condition) **the things your eyes have seen or let them slip from your heart** (condition) **as long as you live. Teach them** (condition) **to your children and to their children after them. 10) Remember** (condition) **the day you stood before the LORD.** NIV

THE HEBREWS' HOUSE:

Suddenly we realize our eternal purpose... we've building a new house where God abides --within ourselves! We are the "many mansions" -- the abiding places! The book of Hebrews discusses our Godly house, **Therefore, holy brethren** (believers)**, partakers of the heavenly calling** (heirs of salvation)**, <u>consider</u> the Apostle and High Priest of our confession, Christ Jesus, who was faithful to Him who appointed Him, as Moses also was faithful in all His house.** (3:2, NKJ). A key to understanding this portion of Scripture is right here. "Consider" or fix your thoughts, mark with attention this thought. What thought? That Christ faithfully endured and still endures. His building did not end, but still continues. He helps all of us build. He completes each building in loving perfection.

Moses built a dwelling in the wilderness, while Christ is the Great Builder of God's house. Jesus is the Apostle and High Priest over that which we profess and acknowledge -- making certain that our confession builds our lives.

Heb. 3:3 **For this One has been counted worthy of more glory than Moses, inasmuch as He who built the house has more honor than the house.** (NKJ) Moses contributed great effort to build a glorious house for God. But, we see a parallelism between Moses and Jesus begin to develop here to add to our understanding. As we interpret the word *house* for this purpose, we note that the Hebrew author uses the illustration of construction.

Heb. 3:4 For every house is built by someone, but He who built all things is God (NKJ). We may do the building, but God built all things. God has greater honor than the house itself. The house, for our purposes, represents us. The beauty of our structure gives all tribute to the architect. Our house can't grow like a plant -- it doesn't evolve on its own, it needs a blueprint. The analogy here says that God is the architect overseeing all the building. God works through the Son (Heb. 1:2, 2:10). Because Jesus builds God's house in us, He is of greater honor than Moses (who built the earthly tabernacle).

Heb. 3:5, And Moses indeed was faithful in all His house as a <u>servant</u>, for a testimony of those things which would be spoken afterward, (NKJ) This is a quote from Numbers 12:7. The Greek word usually used for servant is *dulos*, which means "bondservant." *Dulos* is NOT the word used in this text. Moses was not called a bondslave, slave, or attendant. Instead, the word used here is *therapon*, which means a "noble servant." This word often occurs in the Old Testament, but only once in the original Greek... it represents the unusual relationship that Moses developed with God -- that of a servant of high and noble position.

But, even as great as Moses was, being a servant in the house of God was the best he could ever accomplish. By contrast we see Jesus (Heb 3:6), **Christ as a Son over His own house, <u>whose house we are</u> if we hold fast the confidence and the rejoicing of the hope firm to the end.** (NKJ) Christ was faithful OVER His own house because He was not a servant, but The Son.

Here was see a differentiation between Moses (living under the law) and the believer who's included in the Sonship Company of Jesus. The New Testament house represents His body, His flesh, and His bones (Eph. 5:30). This text verse continues by saying, "whose house we are." Jesus was the Father's house -- and we are the many mansions (abiding places) housed in Him (Jn. 14:2). We belong to His house where He rules.

Individually and collectively we build His house.

"Whose house we are" can also be translated, **"we are God's house."** The metaphor continues to describe us as a house. We are that house if... If what? If we <u>hold fast</u>. This passage introduces the possibility of an unfulfilled condition. The test? If we "hold fast." The Jews of that time had to hold fast through great persecution. They were not to return to the old systems. They had to be "possessors" of God's Word and not merely "professors." Therefore, the mark of a well-built HOUSE is perseverance.

But, let's continue for our purposes, to realize that we may do the building, but God built all things. God has greater honor than the house (your life) itself. The beauty of our struc-

THE KINDS OF WISDOM
Finding the correct wisdom

ture gives all tribute to the architect. Our house can't grow like a plant – it doesn't evolve on its own, it needs a blueprint. The analogy here says that God is the architect overseeing all building. We can't take the credit! God works through the Son (Heb. 1:2, 2:10). Because Jesus builds God's house (tabernacling within us), He is of greater honor.

> "Hold Fast" is a nautical term. This same word is used in Acts 27:40 where it speaks of heading directly toward shore. "Whose house we are" only if we don't deviate or drift from where we're going. If we hold fast to correct concepts and don't drift into false ideologies.

Believers were to confidently hold steady. "Hold fast" to what? Confidence. Confidence (courage) in Jesus proves whether or not you're a true possessor of salvation. We cannot BE A HOUSE unless we have confidence (courage). "With confidence" means that they maintained consistent words and actions that demonstrated and established the fact that they were possessors of the truth. We who are His house display our faith by walking in steady confidence-- no matter what the circumstance.

Plus, these early Christians had another essential assignment in addition to holding fast to the confidant courage. **And the rejoicing of the hope firm to the end.** Rejoicing in hope establishes and verifies a a living witness of one who consistently trusts in the Almighty God. Unto the end – until hope becomes a reality (Rom. 5:2-3, Phil. 3:3). Heb. 10:23 reminds us again, **Let us hold unswervingly to the hope we profess, for he who promised is faithful.**[1]

BUILDING UNTO PERFECTION:

By now the building of our "house" should have moved past having to continuously "repent from dead works." No longer should we be re-learning the "elementary principles of Christ" — over and over. There's more to Christianity than milk (Heb. 5:11). There's more to learn than we know now. There's more growth for the mature to experience, more expanded concepts to realize, and more capabilities to apprehend.

Hebrews 6:1, **Let us go on unto perfection** (*teleiotes*)... The Amplified version explains it further, "Therefore let us go on...advancing steadily toward the completeness and perfection that belongs to spiritual maturity." That idea of *perfection* (*teleiotes*) means completion or finished work, or being grown up. The author of Hebrews urges us to move on past our childhood into the fullness of maturity and completeness-- into present truth -- into a further building of The House.

---

1. Wycliffe Bible Commentary, Moody Press Some comments on Hebrews.

The Happiness of Finding Wisdom

THE KINDS OF WISDOM.
Finding the correct wisdom

Perfection results from the process of aggregating wisdom. Jesus went through that process. Luke 2:39-40 says, **And the child grew and became strong; he was filled with wisdom...** Luke 2:52 **And Jesus grew** (progressively increased) in **wisdom...**NIV

BUILDING UNTO PERFECTION:

By now, the building of our "house" should have moved past having to continuously "repent from dead works." No longer should we be re-learning the "elementary principles of Christ" -- over and over. There's more to Christianity than milk (Heb. 5:11). There's more to learn than we know now. There's more growth for the mature to experience, more expanded concepts to realize, and more capabilities to apprehend.

Hebrews 6:1, **"...let us go on unto perfection** *(teleiotes)*..." The Amplified version explains it further, "Therefore let us go on... advancing steadily toward the completeness and perfection that belongs to spiritual maturity." The idea of perfection (teleiotes) means completion or finished work, or being grown up. The author of Hebrews urges us to move on past out childhood into the fullness of maturity and completeness.

Perfection is the "process" of aggregating wisdom. Jesus went through that process. Luke 2:39-20 says, **And the child grew and became strong; he was filled with wisdom...** Luke 2:52, **And Jesus grew** (progressively increased) **in wisdom...**NIV.

The struggle toward *perfection* is an integral part of the overall restoration process. Ephesians 4:11-13 expands this concept by telling us that the purpose of the five-fold ministries is the perfecting (complete furnishing) of the saints... unto a PERFECT (grown up *teleios*) person..." Those adult individuals are BUILT UP to form a PERMANENT DWELLING PLACE for God in the Spirit..."(Eph 2:21-22), a mature church that walks in unmistakable completeness -- a body that actualizes total redemption.

PERFECT:

Thayer's Lexicon adds that "TELEIOS" means "brought to its end, finished; wanting nothing necessary to completeness; consummate human integrity and virtue; used of men, full grown, adult, of full age, mature." Its root word is "TELOS," which means a definite point or goal; properly, the point aimed at as a limit, i.e. (by implication) the conclusion of an act or state; the end to which all

The Happiness of Finding Wisdom   7-119

THE KINDS OF WISDOM
Finding the correct wisdom

things relate, the aim, purpose." This forceful word defines our coming to full MATURITY in Christ.

This full-grown wholeness manifests itself in clear communications with God, absolute discernment, vivacity for life, unconditional relationships, readiness to subdue difficulty, and an ease in yielding to Spiritual purposes.

God can only have a mature relationship with mature sons.

Each believer must apprehend wholeness (sozo) before he/she is capable of connecting with another. We must grow up before we can discern the singular, consistent divine plan for the church (HIS HOUSE). Paul eloquently explains, **In him the whole building is joined together and rises to become a holy temple in the Lord** (Eph. 2:21). Here we see our individual houses joined to become a temple. But, hear this... it isn't a cute thought for the sweet by and by. It is "joined together" - it is already done! It is a finished work that we must comprehend and apprehend -- the connecting of one to another. It's the valley of dry bones already fused, upright, and walking.

The time has come that the LORD'S house should be completed (Haggai 1:2-5). Permanent charges are eminent. God no longer abides in the temple made with hands — His ultimate purpose is to infuse His nature into the temple of our circumcised heart. This new inundated personality (the PERFECTED *TELEIOS* PERSON) boldly grasps the new concepts received from heaven and resolutely transmits them on wavelengths never before imagined. There's a grand collective truth just beyond our own individual wholeness – that's "US" together.

PREACHING AND MINISTERING WITH WISDOM:

Acts 6:8-11 **And Stephen, full of faith and power, did great wonders and signs among the people...** *And they were not able to resist the wisdom and the Spirit by which he spoke* (NKJV).

Col 1:28 **We proclaim him, admonishing and teaching everyone with all** *wisdom,* **so** (for the purpose) **that we may present everyone perfect** (grown up) **in Christ.** NIV

1 Cor 12:8-9 **To one there is given through the Spirit** *the message of wisdom, to another the message of knowledge* **by means of the same Spirit.** NIV

The Happiness of Finding Wisdom

THE KINDS OF WISDOM.
Finding the correct wisdom

Luke 21:13-19... **But make up your mind not to worry beforehand how you will defend yourselves. For I will give you** *words and wisdom* **that none of your adversaries will be able to resist or contradict.**

THE HAPPINESS OF A DREAM FULFILLED:

In our study of Wisdom, we've seen the necessity of building a good foundation. We've learned that properly responding to life's experiences develops and builds our lives. We know how God's seven pillars should function in our lives. We understand that within our being, we contain Wisdom — THE Person (Jesus) who grows in the garden of our heart. Jesus, our Desire, is the Tree of LIFE that produces godly fruit.

Godly wisdom gives us happiness and produces riches we never dreamed of obtaining. It brings us health (Prov. 3:16) and long life (9:11, 12). It becomes the highway of pleasantness (3:17) with paths of peace.

- Be confident in the walking out of this new direction. God has invested His likeness and image into you. His ultimate purpose is to duplicate His nature in you and to guide you to fulfillment in your unique and personalized life. This process is sacred. There are many others out there also walking their own path toward wisdom.

- As you follow wisdom, you'll begin to walk and pray with increasing power. You will be released upon the world as a witness (Acts. 1:8, & see Col. 2:10).

Slowly, precept-by-precept, wisdom builds our lives. Yes, and life goes on — and on — much like the wheels of the same size within the spinning wheels of Ezekiel's vision. The different aspects of our life interrelate, bringing consistency and symmetry. The various portions of our lives become like the wheels as we inter-relate to reach from the earth to the heavens and connect to the unchanging purposes of God. Selah—

Prov. 8:32-36 **Hear and obey the voice of <u>wisdom</u>! "Now therefore, hearken unto me** (Jesus, the wisdom of God), **o ye sons, for blessed** (very happy) **are they that keep** (watch, guard, protect) **my ways. Hear instruction** (lean knowledge) **and <u>be wise,</u> and refuse** (dismiss) **it not.**

Blessed is the man that heareth (continuously) **me, watching daily** (awake and giving attention to devotional worship and prayer) **at my gates, waiting** (in humble obedience)

The Happiness of Finding Wisdom   7-121

THE KINDS OF WISDOM
The bride has made herself ready.

at the posts (posts on which the door moves) **of my doors. For whoso findeth me findeth life, and shall obtain** (to bring out for use) **favor** (delight) **of the Lord.**

Together WE become the manifestation of His abiding presence.

The clarion cry for Wisdom whistles across the earth. Can you hear it? It vitally stirs the church into action. The day of transformation and the manifested ultimate expression of true Christianity is upon us.

The patterns of Wisdom propel the work of the Lord forward. Wisdom causes us to ascend to new levels of accuracy and unmistakable Christ-likeness. Join me in discovering the unspeakable privilege of disciplining unto godliness — toward the image of Christ Himself. Surely, happy is the person who finds wisdom.

You have given me wisdom and power,
You have made known to me what we asked of you,
You have made known to us the dream of the king."
(Dan. 2:23 NIV)

THE BRIDE HAS MADE HERSELF READY.

The Beginning...

The Happiness of Finding Wisdom

THE KINDS OF WISDOM.
Bibliography:

IBSN 0-9704433-3-1 Copyright applied in June 2000 by
Dr. Kluane Spake
All rights of this book are reserved worldwide.
No part of the book may be reproduced in any
manner whatsoever without giving credit —
except brief quotations
embodied in critical articles or reviews.
No portion of this book may be stored in a retrieval system,
or transmitted in any form or by any means – electronic, mechanical,
photocopy, recording, or any other without permission of author.

BIBLIOGRAPHY:

I believe this manuscript conforms to Copyright laws in America and would be grateful if any unintentional lapses would be drawn to my attention. In addition to the footnotes, much of this book contains ideas of others. To the best of my ability, I've mentioned these authors in the footnotes and/or below. Information (ideas and words) comes liberally from all these sources, sometimes using verbatim apt phrases, sentences and paraphrases. My apologies for any inadvertent lack of documentation. Special thanks to my cousin, the Episcopal Rev. Phillip Baxter and my friend Susan Hart for editing assistance.

- Adams, Jay E. *Godliness through Discipline*, Baker Book House, Grand Rapids, Michigan.
- *Better Living Series*, P.O. Box 5353, Napa, id 83653-5353
- Carlson Learning Company, *"How To Manage Your Time More Effectively."*
- David, Jonathan, *"Developing a Healthy Mind"* Malaysia c 1994 the outline.
- Dayton, Edward R., *"Tools for Time Management"* Zondervan Publishing House, Grand Rapids, Michigan
- Fortune, Doug, *Trumpet Call Prophetic Bulletin*
- Howard, J. Grant, *"Balancing Life's Demands"* Multnomah Press, Portland, Oregon 97266
- Liardon, Roberts, *School of the Spirit,* Creation House, Orlando, Florida
- *"Mastering the Human Mind"* Word of Faith Publishing Co., Dallas, TX 75381
- Soundview Editorial Staff, *"Skills for Success"* Bristol, VT 05443
- Varner, Kelly, *"Proverbs"* Self published, Principles of Present Truth, Richlands, NC
- Veenhoven, Ruut, *"Correlates of Happiness"* 1994 Word database eur.nl/fws/.
- Vos, Howard f., *"Effective Bible Study"* Lamplighter Books, Grand Rapids, Michigan, Zondervan Publishing House.
- Woodroffe, Noel, notes from a lecture.

THE KINDS OF WISDOM
Bibliography:

The Happiness of Finding Wisdom

Printed in the United States
2135